My Cup Runs Over

Family History

ALEXANDER P.
SAMUEL

INDIA · SINGAPORE · MALAYSIA

Notion Press

Old No. 38, New No. 6
McNichols Road, Chetpet
Chennai - 600 031

First Published by Notion Press 2020
Copyright © Alexander P. Samuel 2020
All Rights Reserved.

ISBN 978-1-64587-968-8

Contents

Introduction

This is the true story of my family, as I remember and experienced it- how my ancestors, my parents, my wife and I sailed through the ocean of life. We had lots of challenges but, amazingly, it was solved supernaturally. After years of struggle, we now have a happy life—at the age of our retirement. We were given good parents, good children, and their good spouses, and six God-fearing grandchildren

Happiness is not something readymade; it comes from your own works.

This is the history of my life and my testimony of how the Lord was gracious to me all my life and how the Holy Spirit guided us from time to time. The Lord turned our ancestors from Hinduism to Christianity and saved our entire family from eternal damnation

It is an amazing life experience and my testimony of how God moved us from place to place, like how God moved Israelite Joseph to and from Egypt, to the Holy Land.

Our hardships and moving from place to place were like the family of Lot in the Bible. The Lord saved them from danger of Sodom and Gomorrah. The Lord saved me, from time to time, from similar danger. My life history matches, to some extent, with the Biblical characters of Abraham and Joseph. My life was bitter in the beginning but turned sweet—like honey. God is good. Whoever believes in Him shall not perish but have everlasting life.

Preface

There were many miracles done by the Lord in my life. I cannot even count them because the Lord has performed numerous miracles for an ordinary man like me. He turned me, an ordinary man, into an extraordinary man. I achieved all that I am today through prayers. His grace saved me. He moved me from place to place; He led me on the way to success. I have counted most of the blessings in my life history as a fantastic story of my life.

The Lord's blessings were showered on me so much that "My cup Runs Over" and He was with me all my life, but I was not aware of it.

At the age of retirement, I started counting my blessings. I was amazed that the Lord was so gracious to me. He guided me, led me and helped me when I needed help. God is faithful. The time was ancient. Modern technologies were not there and we lived with lots of hardships and difficulties.

He moved me from one place to another, making accidents or dealing with obstacles in my way, and I was asking: "Why, Lord? Why you have done this to me?" After some time, I could see that the Lord allowed those weird things to me to help me. I now realize that he did all those frightful things just to keep His promises to me—because He loved me.

I was doing well in my business. I was flourishing and I was like a king in the business world of Southern Africa. I was a well-known individual in the business world of Central and Southern Africa. I became the Vice President of the Exporters Association of Botswana and was awarded as the pioneer of the textiles industries and of Indian expatriates, and as the first Indian Christian of Botswana. The Lord gave me more than I deserved. In those days, I thought to myself that I did all that on my own. But I experienced that it was not me; it was the power of my Lord and His Spirit that worked in me, and with me, to achieve what I was and what I am today.

My mother taught me to pray at all times; fasting and praying was key. When I was young, I used to pray just to satisfy my Mum. But when I grew up, it was in my system to pray. The same practice was given to my siblings, as well.

It is unbelievable what our Lord can do for us when you ask him for help. He does not do it instantly, but He does help in His own time and according to His plans. He led me on the way to success. I have counted most of the blessings in my history.

The Lord made me capable in such a way that I never received any wages but I paid wages to thousands of workers. I was not very educated because I had to work to provide for my family in India. My Dad and I had to go through furnaces in life to take care of our family in India.

All my life, I held white-collar jobs; this was a blessing from my Lord. I was always an employer and never employee earning wages. When I was young, I worked as an employee but the wages were not taken; they went directly to my Dad to provide for our family.

The Lord moved me from India to Zambia, from Zambia to Botswana and from Botswana to America. When I was taken from India to Africa, I was depressed from being lonely. But the Lord arranged good people around me and I became happy. When I was taken from Zambia to Botswana, I was very depressed again but it was the Lord's amazing plan for me. Just after I left Zambia, it got dangerous. In Zambia, thieves killed many people in their homes. The person who bought my shop was shot in the shop, by thugs. Amazingly, I was saved.

In Botswana, I could develop my skills, and so, I developed industries and businesses. Botswana was perfect for us but we had to move again, to another country. Only the Lord knew our future. He moved us from Botswana to America. When we settled in America, Botswana was getting dangerous. People were killed in their houses. All the houses had high fences and security devices installed. But still, the houses had burglaries. The Lord moved us from the danger, set us up in safe places and made us comfortable through His mercy and grace.

Today, we are settled in a peaceful and serene house bought by Sylvia and Samir. Our son George, Teena, Angelina and Sanjay are helping in their own way. All our children and their spouses are taking good care of us—especially our youngest daughter, Sylvia, and our son-in-law, Samir, are taking good care of all our needs and comforts. We are blessed; we have three children and the Lord blessed us with six grandchildren. Whatever is called blessings of our Lord, He gave us double portions—just like how He gave Job in the Bible.

Tapestry of My Life

God put my life on a trajectory into the future. He has uniquely chosen me for what I am today. All Christians are called to perfection, and perfection, if defined as an aspiration, is a radical orientation towards living our lives out like Christ lived His. I hereby unfold the secrets of my life, inserting all the details of how Christ worked in my way, while I was away from my parents, brothers and sisters. I am writing all the details as I remember them. As I am shaping up the tapestry of my life, God will revel more and more in me to inspire the readers to live in fear of God at all times, taking lessons from my life history—because God really worked miracles in my life. Everything that happened to me worked out from bitter to sweet—like honey.

When my parents planned to separate to support our large family and send me to Africa to join my Dad, who was already in Africa, I had to sacrifice my happiness and leave all my friends, my mother, two brothers and six sisters at the age of 16—for a long, unknown period of time.

During my departure from home, after the prayer offered by Jane aunty, I said to my mum, with tears in my eyes and fresh flower garlands around my neck—a few moments before my departure—"*Maa*, if I make ten thousand rupees, I will return forever." At that time, the amount was equal to today's ten million. (Ten thousand rupees, today, is $135/-) I started making that money every day in Africa but never had an opportunity to return because as times changed, circumstances were changing and life went on. It was bitter for me at the beginning, but soon, it turned sweet—like honey.

God moved me from Bombay (Mumbai) to Zambia. It was a time when there were no adequate airplane facilities. People travelled by sea. During my teenage, I travelled to Africa by sea and saw the aqua all around me—which was scary at that age.

My Inspiration

To write this life history, I was inspired by my Pastor Dean Barham of the Calvary Chapel of Lighthouse of Manchester; he found my testimony interesting. I have spoken to many friends and they also said that I should write my history because God had plans for me. I thought about it that if I did not write what God did for me, I would be guilty of hiding the blessings God showered on me. I wrote my life history as my testimony—how God saved me from going the wrong way and set me on His path.

I have also listed my genealogy as told by my Dad. It is fascinating to note how my family, in the olden days, lived and moved from place to place. I am blessed and have been successful just because my mother put me on the right path. She taught me how to pray and when to pray. Daily devotions and following strict rules like reading the Bible and going to church without fail were mandatory. I was not allowed to go to my sports matches on Sundays. There was no excuse I could give for Sunday. I managed to pass the same message to my children and they have passed it on to their children.

Thinking about my mum's work in my life reminds me of the first few lines of a book on

Patrice Lumumba, the first President of the Republic of Congo. He wrote:

"If you educate a girl you, you are educating the community; if you educate a boy, you are educating an individual."

I have seen that in my mum and my wife. My mother's teaching was the same as written in the Bible:

Joshua *1:8 "Don't let this book of the law depart from your mouth; meditate on it day and night, so that you may be careful to do everything written in it. Then you will be prosperous and successful."*

When I come across this verse in the Bible, the thought comes in my mind that this is what my mum taught me.

My prosperousness and successes are credited to my mother and my wife.

My Biblical knowledge is credited to my son-in-law, Sanjay Christian, Pastor Claude Stauffer of Calvary Chapel of Hope, Long Island, NY and Pastor Dean Barham of the Calvary Chapel of Lighthouse, Manchester, NH.

My aspirations, my ambition and guidance at every step of life are credited to my dad.

Above all, my success is blessed by the grace of Lord Jesus Christ. The most amazing parts of my life were the miracles performed by Jesus Christ, in His time—the right time, just when I needed them.

I was like Joseph, the son of Jacob, taken away from his own family to Egypt, where he passed through lots of obstacles, problems, suffering and pain. But because the Lord was with him, he became a king in the foreign country. He lived in a foreign country, prospered and helped his family be successful. When I think of the day I left home, I still feel sad. I still hold in my heart that pain and agony, but, though I did not know at that time, the Lord was merciful and He was with me at all times. It was all a part of His plan.

My history is my testimony that God was, is, and will eternally be there for all the believers. Many fools say that there is no God and that it's nature's work in the world. Isaiah's book gives us the correct answer that God is in heaven, sitting on His throne, watching us. The Lord told Isaiah that the people keep on hearing but do not understand; they keep on seeing but do not perceive. I have seen many lost people in this world. They simply do not listen to the words of Jesus Christ.

I wrote a song warning people about the end-time punishment to believers and non-believers.

Heavenly book will be open
When all accounts are done,
Pair of scale of judgment,
Will be in hands of Jesus.
All that you're doing on earth
Is seen by God in Heaven,
Account of every moment
Will be done in Heaven.

Hatia Family/Samuel Family

My name is Alexander—not the great but the greatest. I was named after the great warrior. My uncle Wilson was reading a history book and mentioned that Alexander, the great, was the son of Philip. I was born at that time, so my dad, Philip, named me Alexander. I went through lots of high tests in my life so I think I am the greatest.

God, who created the heaven and the earth, does everything that happens to us and my name is no exception.

I was the only separated black sheep of the family that left home and went to join dad in Africa. My older brother could not go because he was older than the age required by the immigration act. The youngest was too small to go. God chose me to travel to Africa. Being away from my family, I had so much of feelings for them. I used to dream about them in Africa. I used to visualize them going to school, returning and then sitting with mother and praying during the family prayer at 7 PM every evening. I used to see them sitting and eating in front of mum. It was a rule in our house that we did not get breakfast if we did not read the Bible and pray. After a bath, I used to read the Bible and make sure that my mum was looking at me while I was praying. After satisfying my mum, I got breakfast. The rule was much-hated but now, I realize that it was the best rule and every family should have it. The rule kept us religiously good and kept us protected—not only us but also our children.

All the children in our family are God-fearing and attend church regularly. The Lord blessed our family enough to swim through the rough seas of life. All my brothers' and sisters' families are blessed and they are doing well. They lived in acquaintance with each other and do so even now. I feel like I was the only black sheep that was separated from the crowd.

The Hatia Family Name

If you look at the name 'Hatia,' which is my family name, it seems to have originated from the town of Hatia, which is located in the Ranchi district of Jharkhand, in India. The town of Hatia is located on the Indian map at 23°18'N 85°18'E. Hatia is a small town and a railway station. It is adjacent to Ranchi, the capital of Jharkhand. One of the premier technical institutions in the field of metallurgical engineering, the National Institute of Foundry and Forge Technology, is situated there. Hatia developed as a suburb of Ranchi. Away from the rush of the main city, this part of Ranchi is comparatively quiet and calm.

Who knows—our ancestors may have traveled to Bharuch in Gujarat, in the olden days, from Hatia? My Dad told me that his father came from Bharuch to Surat in search of a job. Bharuch to Surat was about 100 miles on a steam-driven train, in the olden days. That used to take about three long hours.

My Grandpa

This is the story of paternal grandpa; I quote again how we faced many challenges in life and they were all only distractions from the enemy to keep us from pursuing our destiny. My grandfather went to Surat to meet three of his friends. The four good friends were also cousins, related to each other on my mother's side of the family. One of the friends had a relative who accommodated them. So, they lived in Rander and they went around looking for a job.

My grandfather found a job with a Christian priest, near a Christian printing press. In India, Christianity started at that particular place, near the Christian press in Surat. A British ship arrived at Surat's docks and started mission work. After the British missionaries, the Irish missioners took over in Gujarat. It was the Irish Presbytery Missionary that started a press near the I.P. Mission Church. The church had a primary and secondary school and a press where they used to print the Bible, the Church's magazines, newsletters and other Christian books. Around the church, there was the mission's compound where all converted Christians used to live. The missionaries had built those houses for them. About 90 percent of the Christians were working at that press. The press is now closed but the church, the Christian houses called the Viswasi Wadi, (believer's garden) and the school still exist. The Irish Presbyterian Mission school is well-known, even now, for good education in Surat.

We are called converted Christians. My Grandpa was Hindu by birth but he was baptized by the Church of Ireland and converted into Christianity. He went through lots of tests in his life. Christian life is suffering. If we accept Christ, we accept suffering and death in Him, and through His precious blood, we are saved. My grandpa travelled from Bharuch to Surat city, a bigger and more prominent city, where the first British ship with soldiers landed and started taking over the Maharajas of India. Ultimately, India became a colony under the rule of England. The British missionaries came in 1816 and the Irish missionaries came after 1841. The missionaries did excellent work in

India. They built lots of big buildings, which still exist. They built hospitals and schools which still speak for themselves.

Under our grandpa, we turned our family from Hinduism to Christianity. Jesus saved and showed us the way to eternity. The Great Commission of Jesus: "All authority in heaven and on earth has been given to me. Therefore, go and make disciples of all nations, baptizing them in the name of the Father and of Son and of Holy Spirit and teaching them to obey everything I have commanded to you." Matthew 28:18–20

My grandpa's name was Samjibhai Jagabhai Hatia (in short, Soma Jaga)

His family originated from Kanthar village, near Bharuch.

My great-grandfather's name was Jagabhai Kika Hatia and he was married to Gangaben Premchand.

They had six sons and one daughter.

The eldest son was Samjibhai, who was my grandfather.

He lived in a small village of Bharuch, about 100 miles from my birthplace, Surat. He had three family friends in Surat: Valjibhiai, Umedbhai, and Silasbhai. They lived in villages around Surat. They were all cousins and good friends.

One of the cousins had family in a village called Rander, about 4 miles from downtown Surat. As soon as he reached Surat, he started looking for a job. Two stayed in Rander while the other two lived in a village called Adajan. They were not educated so they were looking for any kind of job.

The 18th Century

My grandpa worked at Christian missionary, about four miles from Rander. The priest's house was even further from Rander. It was challenging to walk miles through the wilderness every day, so he lived under a tree near the Christian printing press, in the area called "Variavi Bhagol." There, under the tree, he built a hut to have a roof over his head. When he was comfortable and had a well-established job with the Christian environment, he came to know that Jesus Christ is the true God. Grandpa was inspired by the Christian priest to accept Jesus Christ as his savior. The Irish Presbyterian Church baptized my grandpa with the Christian name 'Samuel' from 'Samji.'

The friends, not knowing that now his Christian name was Samuel, still called him Soma (Samji), because he did not tell them that he had converted to Christianity.

The early Christians were like the early Jews who converted in the first century. Though they were converted into Christianity, they were practicing their own religion, like the Jews.

He was acquainted with the Rander village and that is where he found a Hindu girl. My grandpa visited the family often and had more contact with the girl. There was no religious awareness at that time. They did not see any difference because Hindus believed in millions of Gods. He proposed to the girl and married her.

My grandma, Laxmibai Samuel Hatia, was very fair in complexion and was a beautiful-looking girl. Our family and friends used to call her "Lali" (short for Laxmibai) or "Lalima" (honorable name). She married my grandpapa not knowing the difference between her faith and his faith. They had a Hindu marriage. They lived life just like Hindus lived. *Culture does not change by changing faith.*

When she joined my grandpa, she automatically landed in a Christian environment and accepted the so-called English God. She and her family were under the impression that this was another one of the million gods that they worshipped. My grandma was given knowledge of Christianity by the neighborhood. So, she started going to church in the Muglisarah area of Surat, near the Christian press. It was called the Irish Presbyterian Church. Some Gujarati missionaries also taught her some Christian hymns.

I still remember my grandma singing Christian songs. She sang songs on our way to Rander, her maternal hometown. Her best song was in the Gujarati language:

"Bhavsagar ma malio maro Taranhaar, maro Taranhaar."

"Dubto Dekhi Dhasio maro Taranhaar, maro Taranhaar" (*she used to emphasize the word 'Dhasio'*)

English translation:

"I met my Savior, my Savior, in the middle of ocean"

"Seeing (me) drowning, rushed my Savior, my Savior"

She used to emphasize on the word 'rushed.'

She used to take me walking to her maternal village, Rander, through jungle tracks, picking and eating bore berries. There were many berry trees in the wilderness, on the way to Rander. Rander is now a small town; the old beauty of the village has diminished. It is heartbreaking, looking at the old beauty replaced by modern technology.

They lived in the small hut, which my grandpa had built. They were very happy together, living in the area where they had good friends. They had four children—all boys. The eldest was my Dad, Phillip. The other brothers were Emanuel, Simon and Wilson.

Grandpa Travels Overseas

My grandpa and his friends met a sailor who travelled to and from Iraq. The four friends decided to travel to Iraq. At that time, my grandma's brother found a job in a mill near her hut, so he came to live with her. It was then that my grandpa, with his three friends, ventured into the foreign country. The ship's owner was from the Kharva tribe of Aulpad village near Rander. He took them to Iraq on a small ship. They left home not knowing where they were going. The vessel had no facilities in it. It sailed with a sail on a mast that operated manually. The ship reached the port of El-Basra of Iraq after about one month. The ship's owner gave them shelter in El Basra.

A new chapter started for my grandpa. They scattered in Iraq, in search of jobs. Labor-jobs were easy to find in the Arabian country. Very soon, they found jobs in different places. My grandpa found a job in a marketplace, selling vegetables and fruits. The wages weren't great but it was good for a start and it was much more than what he earned in India.

The other friends found jobs in nearby countries. One of them found a job in Abadan, an Iranian city on the Iraq-Iran border. The other friends found jobs in Kuwait, the neighboring country. They were all successful in their foreign ventures.

In a short time, grandpa started his own business, selling fruits and vegetables on a cart.

When he made enough money, he decided to sail back home. He was alone in El-Basra. His friends were very far from each other. My grandpa and one of his friends were well-settled and decided to go back home. They bought tickets to sail back on a slightly bigger ship where they could load their cargo. My grandpa had two big wooden trunks, about four feet in width, three feet in breadth and three feet in height. The Bagdad trunks had heavy wooden outsides and two big locks.

The ship was loaded two days prior to sailing. My grandpa booked two massive trunks with decorated steel bands and loaded it on Thursday, prior to sailing on Sunday.

On Friday, being a holiday in the Islamic country, he took castor oil as a laxative before sailing on the ship, which was to take about one month to reach India. He took it on an empty stomach because he was fasting (our family used to fast every Friday to commemorate Good Friday and the suffering of Jesus) and after that, he had gastro-pains that resulted in a heart attack. He died on Friday night. There was no means of communication to inform his family in India. As per the rules of the Islamic country, he was buried on the same day in a Christian grave in the city of El-Basra, Iraq.

The ship sailed as scheduled on Sunday and reached Bombay after about 30 days. My grandma and all her sons expected to see him arriving on the ship. But on arrival, his friend and a crewmember gave the news about his death.

The situation was grave for my grandma. The friend handed over the trunks to my grandma. The trunks were fully loaded with lots of brass vessels and beautiful chinaware. The cups, saucers, soup bowls, dinner sets, brass pots and brass buckets were lovely. Along with it was lots of clothing for the family and some hidden Iraqi money.

The huge and heavy trunk was placed on the mezzanine floor of our house in Bhutia-Buruj, Variavi Bhagol, in Surat. The trunks were still there in 2009 when I visited the house.

My dad always wanted to go to Iraq to see and pay his respect at the grave. The other friends came with a black-and-white photo of his grave. The grave was near a vineyard. That photo with grapes looming over the grave is still in my sight. I still visualize the picture of the grave of my grandfather. I wanted to fulfill my dad's wish but now, it is dangerous to go to Iraq.

It was dangerous to go there during the time of Saddam Hussein, as well.

Everything changed and the sad part of it is that that none of our family members visited my grandfather's grave. I gave a few Iraqis the full name of my grandfather and asked them to find the Christian grave with my grandfather's full name but the grave was not found. With faith, we know that he is not there. We shall meet him in Heaven, at our Lord's Eternal home.

A Miracle, Our Surat House

Our house in Surat: an unbelievable miracle. God gave us the piece of land to build the house.

My grandma lived in it with her brother, (Manchharam) Manchu *mama*, and her four sons—Philip (my dad), Emmanuel, Simon and Wilson. They lived in a small shack built under a tree. My grandpa was in Iraq, but by God's grace, Manchu-*mama* found a job in a mill near his sister's hut and he came to live with her. There was no income but Manchu-*mama* was helping his sister—my granny. But that was not enough for four children. My grandma and my dad did crochet works. They got metallic threads from a local businessman in Chok Bazaar. They were making metallic laces for the businessman and in return, they used to get some money. It was a good income for them for their everyday life. My dad was so good in doing crochet work that, in Africa, if he saw someone sitting in the neighborhood and working on a crochet, he used to take over and start working on it himself; he was very fast at it. People used to be amazed seeing his quick work. During his young age, it was his daily bread but now, it was just fun and remembrance of the poverty he went through.

Grandpa could not send money from Iraq because there were no bank transfers, bank drafts or check facilities like in modern days. The only way they could send money was through someone going to India, taking money for the families in India.

One day, when Manchu-*mama* was returning from his job at night, as usual, he was drunk. He saw a procession approaching him with lots of lights. In India, those days, it was normal for lanterns to be carried by men on their heads or shoulders, followed by a marriage procession. This particular procession that was approaching Manchu-*mama*, was for an Islamic religious festival called Muharram-Ul-Haram, where they punish themselves by lashing themselves while walking in a procession.

As the procession was passing by Manchu-*mama,* in his drunken state, he stopped by the road allowing procession to pass. At that time, a tall man, clothed in bright white, approached him and slapped him hard. Manchu-*mama* fell down but as he got up, he saw no one around him. The procession was not to be seen and there was no person around him. He was confused and walked home.

That night, Manchu-*mama* had a dream. In that dream, he saw the same tall man clothed in bright white, telling him to go and dig under a tree—he saw this clearly in his dream. He knew the spot, which was near the hut. The next morning, as he woke up, he remembered his dream and told my grandma about the man who slapped him on the road. My grandma obviously did not believe him. She laughed and said that he must have had a little too much to drink the previous night.

However, Manchu-*mama* took it seriously. He went to the tree and dug at the spot he was told to. He knew exactly what he should do. He dug about two feet and found a brass box. It contained some gold coins! Near the treasure, he found a grave. He dug more and found a large grave. He took the money and with it, he bought two pieces of land. He bought one land near the grave and the other exactly opposite his sister's hut.

He built a house of bamboo poles, mud and cow droppings (very common for most of the houses in olden days to be built of cow dung) opposite his sister's hut. The hut where they lived was not on their own land, so the family moved to the new house. The house was built for his sister. His intention was that he would later build another house near the grave. The grave was that of a Muslim person; so, he informed the nearby mosque and its community about it. The Muslim Jamat (community) cleaned the ground and secured the grave; they prayed and painted—whitewashed—the grave.

When I visited the place in 2009—my grandma's house—the grave was still there and the Muslims had built a small room covering the grave.

When my dad and uncles Emanuel and Simon died, Uncle Wilson inherited grandma's house. The Iraqi trunk was still there on the mezzanine floor of the house. Manchu-*mama* died soon after that and no one could build any house on that grave ground as the power of that grave did not allow anyone to build upon it. The villagers were superstitious, too. The place is still empty. Though it belongs to my family, we have abandoned it.

However, the house is now sold to a Muslim family. The Muslim community has taken over the entire area.

My memories of the house are that we used to light up a paraffin lamp every evening. Every day, granny used to clean the glass with some of the ash that goes in the lamp. This lamp gave light to the room. The lantern was good for lighting up the house but one could not read books in the dim light.

I remember we had a great-big wooden swing. Most of the houses had teak wood-based swings, for getting cool air in the summer.

One day, when I was six years old, I was thirsty at night. I got up in the dim light of the paraffin lamp, took a cup full of water and I drank it. Suddenly, I started crying. It was not water in the cup but paraffin. My granny held the lamp's wick high to see more clearly and saw the empty cup in my hand. She realized that I had drunk the paraffin; she screamed. The neighbors woke up and rushed to our house. The people got together and made me vomit out the paraffin.

Anyway, I did not know of that incident. But in 1976, when I visited the area, I visited my dad's uncle's house. Uncle Bartholomew (dad's uncle) died long ago but grandma Ratan-*kaki* was there. She did not recognize me at first but when I told her about my family, she screamed: "Oh, *Ghastelio*" (Paraffin drinker). I asked her all about it and she told me the full story.

It was a nice and cool house. We used to besmear it with cow dung and mud almost every month. The house was rebuilt three times and lastly, it was made into a solid brick house. Electricity and other modern facilities were also there. The only remains of the old memory of that house was the main door of the house. It was made of Teak wood, with carved decorations and steel rings hanging all around it. I saw a similar door in an English pawnshop, priced at 4000 pounds. It was amazing that a four-thousand-pound-worth door was still hanging at my granny's house.

My Dad (Philip Gabriel Samuel)

My dad liked his name, but he did not want to put Samji, Samuel or Soma as his middle name in his school days. So, he selected the name he liked. He chose his middle name to be 'Gabriel.'

I asked him about the name 'Gabriel.' He told me he liked the name Gabriel and so, in school, he wrote his name as Philip Gabriel. He removed the last name, Hatia, too, and placed Samuel—his father's Christian name—as his last name when he left to the foreign country. During his school times, he used to make his own decisions, being the eldest of the family as his father was in Iraq. I go by his last name, Samuel. My younger brother also used Samuel as his last name when he travelled to a foreign country. My older brother, Nelson, and all our sisters kept their last names as Hatia.

After dad's marriage to my mum, Flora, (Fula, Phulbai) they lived in the Bhutia Buruj house; I was born in Surat and lived in that house. However, when I was born, my mum was at her mother Hannah's home. She lived about two miles away from my granny's home. At that time, my dad found a job in Bombay (now Mumbai).

A famous phrase goes: *"My parents are the best parents in the whole world."*

I would proudly say that, again and again. My parents were indeed the best; they were hard-working and devoted to the family.

My mum was in Surat with my granny, her mother-in-law, and my dad found a job in Bombay but could not find a house to stay in. My dad joined the job at the Police Commissioner's office, near a famous place called Crawford market. My dad could not find a shelter for himself so he found a bench in Azad-Maidan (open garden near his workplace.) He slept in the open air the whole night and in the morning; he folded his bedding and kept it at the *Panwala's* (betel-leaf vendor) kiosk shop. The Betel plant is an evergreen Asian climbing plant that is used in the east as a mild stimulant. Parings of areca nuts, lime and cinnamon are wrapped in the leaf, which is chewed, causing the saliva to go red. With prolonged use, the teeth turn black. Some people use a raw-tobacco blend with the cinnamon, as a stimulant.

My dad put his bedding under the kiosk, in a small locker. He paid 5 rupees for a month—a very high rent for those days—for keeping the bedding. In those days, our house rent was just 10 rupees a month. It was the same rent all my life. For his daily bath, he used the same building's water tap and got ready at the back of a restaurant. He lived like that for about two months and with lots of struggle, he found a small room in Bombay's suburb, Elphistone, with the help of a distant relative named Zinna Ghetty. In that building, there was a Muslim family called the Rehamtullas who became very friendly and took care of my dad. Soon, my mum joined my dad. This was the start of our family life in Bombay.

At the office, he was an ordinary clerk at first. But soon after because of his English knowledge at the Irish Presbyterian school, he was promoted to the Commissioner's office. His English knowledge, writing skills and his handwriting were impressive. The Commissioner himself praised him very highly. He was assigned to the Commissioner's office as his personal clerk. He was given the responsibility of handling the Commissioner's confidential matters. He used to do all the work and the Commissioner only signed the documents. He was terrific on the typewriter. There were two reasons for this kind of favor my dad had. Commissioner Bharucha was Parsi and spoke the same language—Gujarati—as my dad. They could understand each other well. Secondly, my dad's writing was excellent—like print on a page. My dad had all the power to write curfew orders and rules given to the police offices of Bombay, under Commissioner Bharucha.

My dad lived by Christian principles and he would not allow any corruption in his department. Many people tried to bribe him but he insulted them and chased them out. One day, I remember that a person came to our house with lots of sweets and firecrackers, during a Hindu festival called Diwali. My dad was furious and sent him back with his gifts. I learnt this lesson on that day and abided by it all my life.

His handwriting and command over English were excellent. He learnt writing with the nib and the holder, used with black and blue ink.

One day, he came home with a ball pen and showed us that this pen does not need ink; it writes without ink. He took a white paper and started writing continuously without using ink! It was a real surprise for us. The ball pen was very precious for us to even touch. Dad kept the ball pen in a glass case. I used to look at it to see where the ink came from. It was a new invention for us. After that, for a long time, I still used ink and the holder with a nib. I had a fountain pen, too, which I used in 1965.

We were members of Ambroli Gujarati Church, a part of U.H.S.M. (Uttar Hind Ni Sayukta Mandali) under the Anglican Church, which later became the Irish Presbyterian mission. (I. P. Mission)

Our priest, Himmatlal Ashirwad, was invited for mission work to Europe. He went to London and Ireland for mission seminars. He boarded a ship, reached London, visited Ireland and took the ship back to India. There were no airplanes in those days. When he returned, we invited him home for lunch. He brought a Parker-brand fountain pen with a gold nib and gave it to my dad as a gift. That pen we never used, because it was too precious to use. Parker and Shaffer pens were too costly and too valuable for an ordinary man to have.

My dad's daily routine was to play with us in the morning. But it was an irritation for us because he used to sing to us every morning, to wake us up. He sang:

"Early to bed and early to rise is the way to be healthy, wealthy and wise."

I kept that in my heart and sung the same for my children and my grandchildren.

Woes of My Father in Bombay

It was a risk for all of us to live without any income. My eldest sister and brother were working as clerks and earned a little, which was not even 20% of what my dad used to earn. My parents were in debt of 3000 rupees to a businessman who had been a good friend and did not demand the money. If we had not borrowed that money, my dad would not have gone to the foreign country. This is also another plan and grace of our Lord—opening foreign nations for us.

This debt would not have occurred, but my Dad wanted to start a small business after resigning from his job at the office of the Police Commissioner of Bombay. It was a prestigious and high position with a good salary and highly-influential work. The entire Bombay police department was under his command. In case of any riots or disturbances in Bombay, he used to pass the Commissioner's orders. He was Commissioner Bharucha's most trusted person.

One day, the Commissioner asked him to go to Delhi with 50,000 rupees. He gave him the money for first-class train tickets and handed over the cash. He was scared to travel with the risk of carrying government money. My dad knew that some of the office staff knew about his travelling with the money to Delhi. He was cautious about the danger. He did not buy the first-class ticket because it was usually a lonely compartment, and someone may attack him. He bought a second-class ticket and hired a coolie (laborer) to get a top deck sleeper for him. The coolie jumped into the train even before it arrived on the platform and occupied a top bunk for my dad. My dad put all the money under his clothing and took a bag with clothing and a sheet for sleeping on the train. When the train arrived at the platform, my dad was already settled on the train. We were looking for him. I was with my mum; we checked every compartment one by one but did not find him. At last, we found the coolie and he showed us where he was sitting. In the second class, he was with lots of passengers so he was very safe. In the morning, as soon as he arrived at Delhi's central station, he rushed out for a rickshaw. He reached the office canteen and had his breakfast, changed his clothing and got ready for the Commissioner. When the Commissioner arrived, he went into his office, introduced himself, handed over the cash to Commissioner and asked him to call Commissioner Bharucha in Bombay. Dad was the only person Commissioner Bharucha trusted the most. Those days, bank-to-bank transfers were not established, as the electronics required were not yet invented. The money was urgent, for some reason. My dad took the risk. If something had gone wrong in delivering the cash, he could have been in jail. When he returned home the fourth day, we were at ease and the tension was gone. Dad was paid a special allowance for the trip.

There was a lot of dangerous work in the department. So, my dad tendered his resignation. When Bharucha received his resignation, he did not want to release him. But dad resigned because of a lot of tension at work; in his own words, 'he used to feel *a sword looming over his head.*' There was lots of craftiness on his assistant's part, who used to instigate problems for him at work while acting as a good friend. He convinced him that he could get better work in well-paying jobs, with all his abilities. The man actually used to accumulate troubles for him so that he resigned and as he was the assistant, he could be promoted to a better position.

Dad was very frustrated. So, he was easily convinced. On a Saturday, at 1 PM, he suddenly came home, announcing that he had resigned from job. The craftiness of the assistant worker had worked, leading him to resign from his 19-year-old job.

There was another intriguing incident that happened; our neighbor, Mr. Sule, who was a palmist, predicted that my dad would resign his job on a Saturday, at 1 PM. My dad took it as joke because we didn't believe in predictions by fortune tellers. But when he came home and said that he had resigned at 1 PM on a Saturday, my mum recalled that this was predicted. Resigning was a mistake, which he realized when the same assistant who used his craftiness, Mr. Mennon—a person, I still visualize with a very dark complexion and a bald head man—took over his position for corruption and to make money. My dad never wanted to do anything against the law. Some people did not like him because he was not corrupt but his assistant clerks used to love him.

My dad had two jobs. He used to take tuition classes to teach children at Mr. Tamane's home. Mr. Tamane had a dairy business. He occasionally used to help my family by giving us good monetary gifts at the time of festivals. He was a Konkani Muslim man with a big heart. I remember attending the wedding of his eldest son, who was one of my dad's students. The whole family respected my dad and honored him throughout.

We were invited to go to his village in Golwaad, near Mumbai. We had very good time with the family and the villagers. We travelled by train up to the Golwaad station and thence by bullock-cart to the village. It was a very fascinating journey. Mr. Tamane had a farm with lots of fruit trees. We ate lots of guavas and mangos at his farm.

After resigning from his job at the Police Commissioner's office, his staff often visited him for help with their work; they were very sad at the loss of a good boss. The man who replaced my dad was incapable of doing his job. The clerks who worked with my dad for a long time used to come to our house and ask for assistance and advice for some tricky problems and my dad helped them solve their problems—for no rewards. Commissioner Bharucha tried to take him back but my dad was not ready for it. He invited my dad to his house and entertained him. He gave him a photo of his for remembrance.

After much thought, when we faced a shortage of money, my dad borrowed some money from a businessman friend and started a small business. He bought an old typewriter and a table and a chair and set up in a kiosk in front of the Bombay Post Head Office. The kiosk was very hot as there was no fan in it. There was a clay pot with a cup over it and a white towel for wiping his face and neck when he sweated. He was self-employed; he worked without any tension but the income was not even half of what he was earning at the police department. I visited him at the kiosk a couple of times and he bought candies and some famous Glucose biscuits; he also sat and ate with me. He stopped eating when a client came in to get some documents done. It was terrible work, but it was much needed for our family's survival. I saw him busy working on his business, but it was not enough. It was tough going and sitting in the heat in a kiosk and the reward was much less than what he used to earn at the Police Commissioner's office. He failed to meet ends. He then searched for a second job and found a part-time job.

He started working two jobs. He found a job at a palace, as secretary and teacher, giving tuitions to the son of the Maharaja. Dhanraj Mahal (the palace) was situated near the Gateway of India. The Maharaja (Emperor) was a very good man but his son was not a good boy. He used to demand a lot of things from his dad. Once, I went to the palace with my dad. There, I saw that the Maharaja's son came to my dad and spoke respectfully, in proper English. He had a small puppy dog, which came near my foot and I became scared that it might bite me. That day onwards, it became miserable for me to go to that palace. My dad was great at the English language so the boy was happy to meet him. My dad used to work for a few hours, checking on supplies, keeping records of the accounts and taking lessons for the boy. That palace is still there in Mumbai—I saw it last in 2017—but it looks like it's turned into a business now.

Dad worked hard at three places at a time but he still could not meet ends with his small income. He was frustrated and applied for a job at the Head Office of the State Transport Company. He was hired immediately and was given the highest position. His salary was better than the one at the police office. He was satisfied and we had a normal life again, but he could not pay his debt to his friend because lots of it had accumulated. He brought the typewriter home and the table and chairs were sold but the debt was still looming over his head. Seeing we had a typewriter at home, Nelson and Violet started trying to learn typing. I was not allowed to touch the typewriter.

My parents had lots of difficulties in providing basic requirements to us and to meet our education expenses. I was taking notes of all the problems my parents were going through.

My dad was a committee member of our Ambroli Gujarati Church, opposite Maharbawadi Police Station, Grant Road, Mumbai. He used to undertake Christmas parcel-making services. It was enjoyable work because we had a Christian neighborhood and a big Catholic church in front of our building. On Christmas Eve, the area used to be very noisy and people were cheerful. They sang and laughed on the street. We worked till late in the night, preparing small gift parcels for all the children at our church to be given after the Christmas service. I remember eating some candies and dry fruits while making the parcels.

Africa Trip's Proposal for My Dad

"It is no secret what God can do!"

This I count as another blessing of our Lord.

After India gained independence, my dad began working at the Police Commissioner's office. But soon after, he resigned his job at the Police Head Office and joined the State Transport Office job. At that time, a businessman came to Mumbai from Rhodesia. He was a relative of one of my dad's friends'. This friend was going to a wedding and could not be in Mumbai on that day. So, he asked my dad to go to the airport and receive the guest. My dad went to receive him at the airport. At the airport, my dad was very well known. He received the man, named Mr. C. C. Patel, at the port with no difficulties. This man was very impressed with my dad, his fluency in the English and Gujarati languages and his influence over the airport authorities. He asked my dad to come to Africa and join his business; he promised him excellent rewards.

After returning to Africa, Mr. C. C. Patel sent tickets, travel-related documents and money to my dad, to go to Africa. My dad's mum and my granny were reluctant to let him travel to a foreign country. So, my Dad took unpaid leave for three months from the workplace and decided to travel to Africa. I remember that he was looking for a suitcase for his journey. He came home with an old, red suitcase made of leather. I don't know where he picked it up from—I suppose from Chor-Bazaar, as it was very famous for such old items. He filled the suitcase with his clothes and got ready to travel.

My Dad's Voyage to Africa: 1952

The day of his separation from his wife and nine children—without any income or savings—my dad boarded a British-Indian steamer named S.S. Amra. We knew we were going to face difficulties because the breadwinner had left and we did not know what would happen if he didn't make it to Africa. It was a risk for all of us to live without an income. We were praying that God would provide for us.

At this point, today, I am reminded of a Hindi film's song. I saw the film in Johannesburg, South Africa when I went to visit—on business—a handbag factory. The theater was under the hotel. I heard that song in that film and wept a lot. I kept wiping my tears and watching the film. I remember the name of the Hindi film—*Takdeer*. The song goes like this:

(Hindi words)

Saat Samunder paar ker ke, Gudio ke bazaar se, Achhi si gudia lana, Gudia Chahe Na laana, Pappa Jaldi aa Jana.

(English translation)

Across the seven seas, from the doll market, get one doll for me, If not possible, don't bring the doll but Pappa come soon.

We were in the same situation when our *Pappa* left us. I asked my dad for a gold belt for my waist. My dad laughed and said, "Yes, I will bring one made of pure gold." I still visualize the place where I spoke to him and my dad laughing at me. I dreamed about it too.

On S.S. Amra, he met a Gujarati farmer's young sons, going to the same destination. My dad saw that they were reading books. He looked at the books—they were reading primary-school-level English books. He asked them, sarcastically, what language it was. They said this was called English and that they had to know the English language, because, at the Northern Rhodesia border, there would be an English test. My dad told them that he had no book and asked if anyone could teach him. They all studied together and tried to help teaching my dad English. My dad was just teasing them because he was very good in the language.

When they reached the border, a European Immigration officer sat for the test. He had a cheroot in his mouth and spoke to them, asking them to write a ten-line essay on a bicycle.

My dad wrote it in five minutes and sat waiting for the others to complete. They were given half an hour to write. At the end of the time, they all looked at my dad with sympathy and thought that the man would fail. When the test was completed, they found out that, out of 30 people, only my dad had passed. They were surprised and asked my dad about it. My dad said that he did not write anything, so they'd sympathized with him and made him pass.

Anyway, they were given a one-month entry for the second test. The company's boss, Mr. C. C. Patel, knew my dad's capabilities; so, he asked him to train the crowd for the next tests in that time.

From that day, my dad became very popular in the city, among the Indian community—because he was the only one with good English knowledge and was good in, both, Gujarati and English—and had writing, speaking and teaching skills.

In Africa, he worked for Mr. C. C. Patel's wholesale distribution private firm. The company was called C. C. Patel and Company. He earned 30 Sterling Pounds a month as salary. He was given free accommodation and free food. He hardly spent any money on himself. He used to send 29 pounds to my mum and kept only one pound as his savings.

When the first draft arrived at our Mumbai home, the expressions on my mum's face were seen by me but cannot be explained. She was so thrilled that she went straight to the Bible and started thanking the Lord for the rescue.

Thereafter, every month we received bank drafts and our life became normal and worry-free. My mum started paying the accumulated debts.

Today, as I write this, 3000 rupees is a tiny amount for any family in India. But in those days, it was huge debt for us. The average income of the biggest officer in any government department was about 400 rupees per month—maximum—and my dad used to get more than that. Yet, the huge family could not survive comfortably in that income.

Working for C. C. Patel and Company was a good start because it gave immediate relief to our family from our poverty. My mother could repay all the debt in a short span of time. All my brothers and sisters were comfortable and doing well in their studies.

In 1955, my dad managed to get an entry permit for me. I was given an opportunity to join my dad. I was with my dad in August 1955. I saw how my dad was struggling and working hard for the family. Soon after my arrival, my dad left C. C. Patel and Company because Mr. Patel died and his shareholders took over.

Dad then joined a customs-clearing agency. There was a member of our church, who offered a job to my dad. It was a better-paying job, but he had to rent a home and cook food for himself. He took up the challenge started working for Mr. Macleod.

My dad could not work at the office because of color discrimination. White firms were not allowed to employ non-white employees for office jobs.

The company gave him a room inside the parking area of the transport trucks. It was a nice, small office, partly turned into a home. There were a few toilets in the parking area for the transporters but we kept one of them locked for ourselves. We used to get up early, at 5 AM, and bathe in the darkness, before dawn, on the steps of the office. It was a struggle but to provide for our growing family, we had to struggle.

For food, we faced big problems because we did not have a cooking range; we did not have money to buy a stove and there was no place for it. There was a heater in the office; we used the coil heater to heat bathing water in the morning. After that, we used to make tea for ourselves. For lunch, we had only one menu—rice and moong bean soup—everyday. There was no control switch on the heater so we used to boil the rice and drain the extra water out. We boiled the moong beans to liquidize it, spiced it slightly and ate it with a good slab of butter, for taste. We had no choice but to keep smiling and enjoy the food—the rice and moong soup, daily. Evening's dinner, however, was the same soup with bread. This was our daily food. It was hard but occasionally, people used to give us a few rotis (Indian homemade bread). We used to walk home fast to eat the rotis fresh—before they got cold. We used to eat them with the same moong soup. Sometimes, during weekends, some Muslim and Hindu families used to invite us over for dinner.

When we ate at someone's home, whether the food was good or bad in taste, whether it was too spicy or too salty, we always praised the food. Likewise, nowadays, when my wife cooks food and forgets to add salt sometimes, I never complain about it. When she eats after me, she immediately says, "Why did you not tell me that salt is less in the food?" I always say, "The food was excellent." It had become my nature.

When I got married and my wife asked me to get bread, I refused to eat bread because I had had enough bread in my early life. When I explained my previous menu to her, she stopped asking for the bread. For a while, I hated bread. I still remember the Waddle Bakery, where we bought our daily bread in Ndola, Zambia.

My dad had lots of problems working in the hard conditions. So, he found a job at a new Company named CAMCO (Central African Marketing Company). In that company, my dad had to travel long distances. He was given a car and a driver. The driver's name was Muhammad; he was of East-African origin and became very good friends with my dad. He took good care of my dad. He was a good mechanic, too. They travelled long distances, mostly by road.

One day, Muhammad and dad were travelling from Broken-hill (Kabwe now) city towards Ndola, when they met with an accident. The Peugeot Station Wagon's front tire burst and the vehicle somersaulted a couple of times before it stood on the side of the road. Those days, cars did not have safety belts. Fortunately, they escaped with very little injuries. Muhammad changed the wheel and travelled to the nearest city. The station wagon, with all the commodities and sample boxes, could have injured their neck or back but there was a heavy mesh between the front and the back storage compartments. God is great; my dad used to start his day with prayer. My mum prayed for us every day. Prayers saved us from so many mishaps.

My dad lived in a friend's—Mr. Dhirubhai's—house where he had food also. The work at CAMCO was very hard and involved lots of travelling. It was too much for my dad's old age, and so was the danger on the road. Dad could not do it anymore. So, he left the job.

After leaving CAMCO, my dad worked as the Managing Director of a company called Rhodger Sales Company of Bulawayo, Southern Rhodesia (now Zimbabwe). The Director and Chairman of that company was Nettie (Nathan) Gershman.

Gershman joined the names 'Rhod' (Rhodesia) and 'Ger' (Gershman) and called the company Rhodger Sales. Mr. Gershman was a Jewish gentleman with very good business acumen, and kind hearted. My dad was the Director of the Zambia branch. That was the last company he worked for.

At that time, dad was planning to buy a farm in India. He could not buy farm in India because he had no farming experience. He told me to obtain a certificate stating that I had over five years' farming experience in Zambia. I had a farm in Lusaka on my little brother Augustine's name. The lawyer was a good person; he got me a certificate saying that I was a farmer. My Dad came to Lusaka, and I gave him the certificate and 1000 British Sterling Pounds for the farm. This was hard-earned money from our Lilayi shop, which was kept in our house as savings.

The History Given by My Father

I would have not known my family's history but it so happened that my Dad fell sick with prostate gland issues. He had trouble with it when he came to meet me at my factory in Botswana. He came from the factory's restroom and told me that he must see the doctor because he could not pass water. I took him immediately to the hospital where a Taiwanese doctor was my good friend. He was walking to the minor surgeries clinic. I stopped my car by his side and asked him for help. He immediately took dad and helped him pass water. My dad came to me after about 20 minutes and said that the doctor did not charge anything. I said that he would not charge me anything because he was my good friend. When I heard about his prostate problems, I got to know that he was suffering for a long time.

I was in Botswana when he was sick. His assistant, Mr. Rafik Burhani, took him to the Ndola main hospital. His wife, Kubrakhanam-*chachi* cooked healthy food to feed my dad at the hospital. I would like to note here that their daughter, Farzana, who is married in Navsari, India, was good help when dad was in the eye hospital in Navsari, India. Both, Farzana and her husband, delivered food to my dad on a heavy monsoon rainy day. Dad did not expect them to come because it was raining heavily but they were so kind and caring that even in that heavy rain, they walked in knee-high floodwater in the darkness of the night to deliver the food. My dad mentioned this again and again to me, for such love did Rafik Burhani uncle's family have for us.

Rafik-*chacha*—the name I used to call him—used to visit us in Lusaka but he never had any food at our house because he suffered from diabetes. Farzana and her husband came to our home in Valsad, during my dad's funeral, and stayed there with us till late like our own family members. This is the kind of love people gave us. I cannot forget it and cannot refrain from mentioning it in my history.

Dad was alone, working as a Managing Director. He had his two Indian assistants and two African staff. My dad used to stay with Dhirubhai's family in Ndola, Zambia. I had usual communication with my dad, at least once a day. Phone calls those days were a little difficult to make because of the STD lines—and my phone was on party lines. I could call him from my office and he used to call me from his office. Rafik-*chacha* gave me the news that my dad was in the hospital but he was fine. He used to visit him every day.

It so happened that my dad was taken to the imaging room for his X-ray before the surgery. The nurse came and took him to the room, took his clothing off and gave him a sheet for the X-ray before waiting for the X-ray operator to come. The man did not come because it was lunchtime. The nurse left him in the room and walked away for lunch, thinking the man would come. My dad was in the fully air-conditioned room for more than an hour and a half—till the nurse remembered that she had left a patient in the X-ray room. She came in and found my dad shivering with high fever. She took him to his room and covered him with a warm blanket. My dad became very sick and so, it was not possible to have the surgery for about two weeks—till he got back to normal health.

I called the office, as usual, and spoke to the African staff. He rebuked me and said to me: What kind of son you are? Your father is very sick and he refuses to have surgery." I was shocked; I did not know that my dad was that ill. Everyone said he was fine and was doing well, but only this man told me the real story.

I jumped in my chair and contacted my wife. I asked her to come to the office and take care of the office. I then drove to the airport and asked for a ticket for Ndola, Zambia. There were no flights going to Zambia that day, but there was a flight going from Livingston (Zambia) to Ndola. I was helpless but then I found a chartered flight with a pilot ready to fly me to Livingstone. I hired the chartered flight and, in two hours, I reached Livingstone—just in time to board the flight to Ndola. I contacted Dhirubhai Naik, the gentleman with whom my dad lived. I reached Ndola at about 4 PM.

I reached the hospital with Dhirubhai and Rafik-*chacha* and found that my Dad was fine but had a urinary bag connected to him. He told me the experience he had at the X-ray room. He told me that he did not trust these people as they had funerals every day. He said that they would kill him, too. I went straight to the doctor in-charge of the hospital.

He was a gentleman from Delhi, working on a contract at the hospital. He told me they did not have medicines in that hospital. He told me that it was difficult to treat people there. I realized that it was not safe to be at that hospital. So, I asked for the doctor's permission and got the release papers and other documents signed. I had to take the instant decision of sending my dad to India for surgery. I told my dad that I was sending him to India. He was very happy and gave me a big smile.

I called my travel-agent friend in Lusaka and asked him to issue our tickets to travel to Lusaka, and a ticket for my dad to Bombay. The tickets were ready. I asked my older brother, Nelson, who was in Lusaka, to pick-up the tickets from the agent and meet us at the airport.

In the morning, I picked my dad up from the Ndola hospital and went straight to the Ndola airport. The flight to India was available from Lusaka International only. So, I flew with him to Lusaka. On the Ndola-Lusaka flight, he was partially conscious. He started speaking about his family's history and told me about his family, the hut, Manchu *mama* and many other amazing things. I heard all this and kept it in my mind. At that stage, I was more worried about his health than his past.

When we reached Lusaka airport, I contacted the ground staff to get him a bed for his comfort. They took us to the sickbay at the airport. There, the resident nurse gave him a very comfortable bed and blanket and my dad took good rest. I was sitting by him and he continued his history. I remember the history he gave me in our quiet hour at the airport's sickbay.

At that time, Nelson and his wife, Kusum-*bhabhi,* came with some food and the tickets from my agent—for Dad to travel to Bombay.

I was given permission to take my dad with the wheelchair to board the plane. I made him comfortable in the last seat of the plane and gave him sleeping pills.

He reached Bombay in the morning. At the Bombay airport, a crowd of people came to see my dad. My brother-in-law, Dr. Wilson Parmar, arranged for an ambulance to take him to a hospital in Bombay. I called my mum that day and she told me all about his journey. He was still sleeping on the flight when Dr. Wilson reached us inside the plane. The ambulance was ready at the steps of the aircraft. They went straight to the hospital. My dad had a safe surgery and he was delighted to be with our family.

My Dad's Retirement

My mum wrote a letter to my dad in poetic words.

Dad read the letter; he gave it to me and said: "Read this." My dad looked sad reading the letter. I read it and wept internally. That was a time when I was still in Zambia and Nelson was still in India. It was too early for my dad to return home because he did not have any savings—but I had my mind set on getting my dad to retire as soon as possible. I could figure out that my mum was missing my dad. It was almost about 15 years of separation for them.

My mum's words were:

Actual words in the Gujarati language:

"Apna Jiven ni sandhya avi gayi chhe, mate raat pade te pehla pachha faro"

English Translation:

"The evening of our life is here, return home before it gets dark."

The Lord started moving for me. Jesus did weird things to set me on the right track. I always used to speak to Him, saying, "Why, Lord? Why am I in such jeopardy?" Jesus knew the future. The Zambian government did not give me citizenship, so I had to go to the British High Commissioner's office in Lusaka to get my citizenship of the United Kingdom. It was a British Overseas Citizenship. So, if I needed to go to Britain, I'd have to obtain a visa to enter. The passport said 'British Overseas Citizen of Rhodesia and Nyasaland.' The British passport allowed me to travel freely to other parts of the world.

Immediately after getting my British passport, the Lord answered me as to why he did not allow me to get a Zambian citizenship. My changing of nationalities was in March and thereafter, in May, the President of Zambia, Dr. Kenneth Kaunda, nationalized 31 key companies overnight and cancelled all the licenses of all non-citizens who had shops in the rural areas of Zambia.

I was affected by that law and had to close my shop. I was given time up to December 31. In the meantime, Nelson arrived with Irene, from India. I had no shop but I did salesmanship and travelled from Lusaka to Livingstone every week. I earned a sales commission from the goods I sold. I had to give up my business in Lilayi. The shop was closed and my salesmanship was going well but it was not enough to live on in the long run.

When Nelson came with the intention of settling permanently, I had to apply for a residence permit for him. If I applied for his Work/Residence Permit, Nelson would have to go out of the country. So, I arranged to send him to Dar Es Salam to stay with a good friend—a top businessman of Tanzania, Mr. Laljibhai Mehta of Tanzania State's clearing agency. Lalji Mehta controlled all the imports and exports of Tanzania. Besides taking care of my sales business, I had to approach the Department of Home Affairs on a daily basis. This became my daily routine—I approached the department every day to get the resident permit in time because the permit's processing may take three to six months and it may also be denied. I had to pay some officers and request that a quick job be done. I must praise the Lord for, through His mercy and kindness, the permit was issued in one month. I obtained the residence permit and asked Laljihai Mehta to send Nelson back to Zambia. When Nelson arrived in Lusaka, my dad was very happy. Dad flew from Ndola to Lusaka just to meet Nelson and Irene.

Dad came to meet Nelson and asked him to apply for jobs. Dad wrote an application format for him to follow and write to all the advertised jobs. Nelson wrote many application letters and sent it to various places. He wrote so many applications that he memorized the letter. In the meantime, the Lord's amazing grace poured on us. One of my friends offered to give him a job. I took Nelson to the owner of an insurance company. The first question he asked was about Nelson's English knowledge. I told him that his English was good. He then said to Nelson to write an application for the job. This was very easy because Nelson wrote tons of applications and had memorized the letter's format well. He wrote the application in five minutes and handed over the paper to him. He was impressed that Nelson wrote a grammatically correct letter—one that was written so fast. He employed him immediately.

Nelson was now set with a job and was-settled in Zambia. I was assigned to go to Botswana to start a new chapter of my life. I left my wife, Irene and Augustine in Lusaka and travelled to Botswana. The house was a rented one so I paid the rent from my bank account—the rent got paid automatically every month.

Anyway, with lots of difficulties, the Lord helped us establish Nelson in Zambia. I was assigned to go to Botswana to start a new factory for a Zimbabwe-based South African company. I had newly established work as the Managing Director of the company.

I took Irene, my wife and our son, George, to Botswana. I was not yet set-up properly in Botswana but I started a hat factory for Mr. Gershman and his partner, Hyman. I had lots of difficulties settling down in primitive Botswana and the new hat factory.

Many white South African people were surprised to see me having a permit. The resident permit to enter Botswana was not for the non-whites. The country had just got their independence. The government was nationalized. The clerks were African citizens from Botswana but the bosses were still South African whites with a discriminative policy. It was only two years since Bechuanaland had become a newly-independent country with a new name—Botswana.

Botswana was under the British but it was still under the protection of South Africa, which still had color-discrimination rules. Bechuanaland (now Botswana) was called a British protectorate country. The South African government was taking care of the administration of the country. The Lord moved for me and got me my residence permit. Because my name was Alexander Samuel and I was holding a British passport, the authorities thought that I was a white British man. But, when I arrived in the country, they found that a black British man had arrived. I employed an electrician to do the electric work in my new factory. He was working at my factory when he found that I was an Indian and not a colored man from South Africa or Botswana. He asked me how I got my permit and where I'd learned hat manufacturing from. I never had any training; I only saw the factory operations in Johannesburg, South Africa but I couldn't say that to him. I bluffed and answered him that hat manufacturing was in my blood; that it was our family business and that is why our family name is Hatia (hat-maker). He was convinced but it was not the truth. From Francistown, Botswana, I sent my wife to India, accompanying Irene and George. My wife was pregnant and expecting our second child. When they left, everyone from the Indian community of Francistown (originating from South Africa) came to the airport to bid them farewell. There were about 20 people who came in honor of my family. Those days, all family members had love for my family. In a short time, I had earned the friendship and love of the families in Francistown. Let me quote that they were all Muslim families that loved us so very much. The airport was very small and there was only one flight a day, besides chartered flights.

Nelson was well-settled in his job. He lived in a fully-furnished house and I paid the rent for it. I had sufficient bank balance and income from my properties in Zambia.

My wife had a good time in India and returned back to Lusaka. She had to go to Lusaka because there were no adequate facilities in Francistown and I did not have much idea about the maternity facilities in the town.

I Praise the Lord that during the last days of her pregnancy, my sister-in-law—my wife's elder sister—came to Lusaka from East Africa, where she and her husband were working on a temporary basis. My wife had a lot of help and support when Angelina was born.

In December 1970, I closed my factory for Christmas vacations. I drove with Dr. Shibley to Zambia as he wanted to tour the place.

After the Christmas vacation, I took my wife and both our children to Botswana, leaving the house with my brothers Nelson and Augustine.

In 1972, my mother-in-law and sister-in-law came for a visit. They were delighted to be in a foreign country. At that time, our third daughter, Sylvia, was born. They took care of the children and my wife. God was always gracious to us that we were not left alone when we needed help. When Sylvia was one year old, I sent the family to India on a ship. My mother-in-law wanted to see Karachi and meet her family at the Karachi seaport. They met each other for the first time since 1947, when they were separated during the partition of India and Pakistan. They could not go out into Pakistan with their Indian passports, so they met at the ship.

I travelled by flight to India because I had a limited vacation. I flew to Bombay and reached earlier than them. At the Indian port, I went to receive my family. My children were confused and said, "We have one *Pappa* in Africa and one in India, too."

Thereafter, my parents started arranging my younger brother Augustine's marriage.

After a few months, Augustine came to India and got married to my sister-in-law, Edna (Manorama) and went to the USA.

Some years later, my mum and my little sister Mabel (Bimba) came from India to visit us. My dad also came from Ndola to accompany them for some time. At that time, I was settling down in Botswana. I had a great time taking them on a tour of Zambia, Botswana and Zimbabwe.

Mabel left for India because she had to be there in time for her college. Soon after, unfortunately, dad became very sick. He had double pneumonia and was hospitalized in Francistown Hospital. The hospital's doctors-in-charge and staff knew me well. They took excellent care of dad but dad did not respond to the antibiotics. At that time, when I went to see dad on a Monday morning, I passed by the X-ray department where our church's assistant priest was working. He saw me passing by, stopped me and said to me, "Your dad is in a very serious condition; take him to Bulawayo Hospital immediately."

I took immediate action. I took the X-ray and the doctor's report in 10 minutes and arranged for going to Bulawayo city with a friend to drive for me, because I was shaky. I called the immigration officers on both sides of the Botswana-Zimbabwe border about my emergency passing through both the borders. Both borders' officials were waiting for me to pass without clearing immigration and customs procedures. We reached Bulawayo's Mater-Dai Hospital at about 11 AM. My dad was now very sick so I went to the Emergency. At the emergency ward, the head nurse, (A Roman Catholic nurse who was in-charge) saw the X-ray and the reports. She rushed him to the room and started his treatment. At the same time, she called Dr. Shea, who was the best physician in Bulawayo.

Shortly, Doctor Shea walked into the ward. He did not greet anyone; he went straight to the patient, connected all the necessary equipment and injected the antibiotics and IV. He kept doing his job for at least an hour. After doing all the necessary work on my dad, he came to meet us. He spoke to us, saying that my dad had only a 30% chance of survival. He said that if he breathed safely that night, he may have a chance at survival. My mum was stunned; she did not speak. She did not move from his bedside and wept internally. She kept praying. I tried to get her out from there but she refused to move.

I went out to pray at the hospital's chapel, on the 5th floor. The chapel was empty; I prayed, but could not concentrate. So, I came out, sat on a bench outside of the chapel and went in again to pray. I knelt down on a cushion in the front bench but I still could not concentrate. I must have done so several times before I was finally at peace, kneeling down. I wept and then sat on the bench, looking at the cross. Soon after, I came out and said to my mum that dad would be okay and that there was nothing to worry about.

The doctor was gone and it was already 6 PM. So, the nurses, who were by dad's bedside from 11 AM, did not move even though their shift was over. They said that they would work extra hours and take care of my dad. These were the fantastic contributions of those Catholic nurses.

Many friends and staff, and our business directors came to meet us.

They all tried to comfort us and offered help.

We were given Serimontil, a sedative medication, to calm us down and help us sleep well. I was planning to go to the hospital at 5 AM but I slept till 8 AM. When I woke up, I rushed straight to the phone and spoke to the nurses about my dad. One of the two nurses attending my dad came and said that dad was breathing normally; she asked me not to worry. My mum also got up late that day and we went to hospital to see dad. The sedative worked—it gave us good rest. We reached the hospital. The doctor was not there then, but at about 10 AM, he came to see my dad. He said to me that dad was okay but not yet conscious.

Dad was kept in a private room for special treatments. Doctor Shea said that he would not recognize us and that it would take time for him to get back to normal. Doctors told us to not go to his room and to keep away from him. We didn't dare go inside the room. He was kept in a private ward. If we went in and if he had come to know that one of us had come, he may have had problems. So, we did not see him but just peeped through the door hinge's gap.

It took one month for dad to come to his senses. He started to recognize us and started speaking to us in a frail voice. Praise the Lord for he heard my prayers. We took dad on a wheelchair in the hospital garden to give him fresh air, and he got better day-by-day. He was discharged from the hospital and we came back to Botswana.

Dad's Imminent Retirement

My mum initiated the discussion about dad's retirement. I could see that she was missing him and it was about time that my dad retired. I told my dad that he must return home. He was reluctant because he had no savings. I offered him all my property and my savings in Zambia. I told him to sell all the property and take the total funds from my savings account and return back home. Both my mum and dad were very happy with my offer, but then he said that the exchange control regulation in Zambia would not allow transferring all the money.

I told him to go back to Zambia, sell all my property and take all the money from my account and deposit it in his Barclays Bank account in Lusaka. He said to me that he would need a monthly income in case the money transfer to India took time. I promised to transfer a certain amount to him for his monthly expenses.

The next day, I took him to my bank—Standard Chartered Bank in Francistown, Botswana—and signed standing orders to transfer money every month, automatically, from my account to his account at Grindlays Bank, Mumbai. He was very pleased and with much joy, he told my mum all about what I'd done for him. My mum and dad gave me their abundant blessings from the bottom of their hearts. I did not have much income in Botswana at that time, but I did not show my dad my problems.

The exchange control regulation did not allow me to transfer any money to my savings account because, as a rule, they allowed only 50% of my income to be transferred. Dad was getting funds from my account already, so I had problems because I could not go out on vacations without money—but I could go to South Africa.

My dad sold all my property through a South African-Indian lawyer in Lusaka. The lawyer asked me to come to Lusaka to finalize the deals. I met the lawyer and paid him his fees first. Then, I collected all the checks and handed them over to my dad. I transferred all my money from my account to his Lusaka account and closed my account in Zambia.

Nelson was getting rent from my account—that stopped. At that time, my brother was well-settled and his family had also joined him. My sister-in-law was working, so they were well-settled in Zambia.

I started my life in Botswana with very little income because I was still developing my business for the Zimbabwe-based company. I started my life with lots of struggles but kept all that to myself.

Dad returned to India, taking some money with him—only that which was allowed by the exchange control regulations. He had deposited all the money in Barclays Bank, Lusaka, Zambia. He put the remaining funds in the pipeline by setting installments from the bank to be made directly to his Grindlays Bank account in Mumbai.

Dad Returned to India

My Dad worked hard all his life just to provide for the needs of our family. He returned with full confidence that he was financially safe. I saw my mum and dad—they were very happy and I feel like that was my reward.

My dad was on the move in India. The first thing he did was sell my house in Borivli, the last suburb of Mumbai. I had bought a five-bedroom house in front of a garden on Chandaverker lane road, from where the station was a five-minute walk. He was given wrong advice by someone that, according to the emergency law of Indira Gandhi's, I may have to lose my house. My dad was convinced that because I was not a resident at that time in Mumbai, I couldn't have a house on my name. The house was sold for one lakh (100,000) rupees only. I was not informed. The deal was done and the money was taken. When I visited Bombay to visit my parents, my dad casually informed me that the house was sold. I told my dad the value of the house, in just a year, would be 500,000 rupees (five lakh).

He agreed that it was his mistake. Five years later, the house was worth 50,00,000 rupees (fifty lakhs) and even then the owner would not sell it—even for two crores (twenty million).

I believe that the Lord did it for a purpose. As Apostle Paul wrote, 'We are afflicted but not crushed, perplexed but not driven to despair, struck down but not destroyed.' The Holy Spirit was guiding us in His way, and we followed the Lord's plan. We are remaining in the power of the spirit of our Lord. I did not say anything to my dad because he did what he thought was best for us. All the good or bad that happens to us is the plan of our Lord.

Dad was on the move again; he bought a farm—which was about 200 miles away from our Bombay home. This farm was bought according to the plan we made in Africa. I handed over the certificate that I had made in Zambia, which stated that I was a farmer over there, to my dad. In Botswana, we had accumulated 1000 Sterling Pounds for our savings, which was given to dad. He bought a farm and suffered the tough farm life—with heavy rains, the cold, the heat and many other farm-related problems—before he realized that it was not for him. He was not a farmer; he had made a mistake again. He tried to live like a farmer but he failed. Ultimately, he sold the farm. I was not informed about that, too. He then returned to our home in Bombay.

My mother was relieved because she was against the farm idea from the very first. The farm was not important to me, my mum's satisfaction was.

My dad could not stay idle. When I visited him in Bombay, I had a good talk with him. He wanted to be busy. I didn't blame him because all his life, he had been busy working. I realized that he was businessman in Africa. So, I told him to supply goods to me for my business—just to keep him busy. He started that, too. I gave him names of the suppliers. He contacted them and began supplying goods to me. But then, he began planning to build a house for the family. He stopped the supply business because it was too much of a hassle for him, at his age.

My father was on the move again. He bought a house in Vadodara city, which was not good for the family because my mum did not want to leave Bombay. The house was getting ready but my mum was not happy about it. Shortly after, they sold the Vadodara house.

Dad started another project. He wanted to build a house for the family. He chose to buy a plot for building a big bungalow for the family. It was his dream that all his children come live with him during their vacations. He purchased a plot in a residential area in Valsad, about 250 km from Bombay. He wrote to me that it would cost 2,50,000 (two and half lakh) rupees to build the house. He was always up to something. He asked me to send money for the construction. I started looking for someone who could send money by taking a 10% commission from me. Mr. Gyan Singh, who was in the Botswana Army, helped me send some money while making a 10% commission from me. He had a good relationship with my dad. I sent money again through a lady doctor in the army, whose father was an Indian Army Colonel, in Poona. Likewise, I sent money through teachers who were on contract, while paying them a 10% commission. I sent enough money to build the house. Some more money was still wanted; so, my dad wrote to me, asking me to send some money for the construction. I arranged for a draft from London Bank to help with finishing the house. My dad received the money and he completed the house in Valsad.

The house-building put me in jeopardy—arranging for funds from Botswana, friend's connections and paying commissions to them and my London account.

Valsad is about 250 km from Mumbai. My mum was not happy about moving into that small town, leaving the huge city of Mumbai where she lived all her life. But my father thought we should have better standards of living. The big family house was getting ready.

Six months before the completion of the house, my mum died suddenly—due to a massive heart attack! The happiness of our family turned into sorrow. The dreams of my dad were shattered. I received a phone call from Mumbai, in Botswana, at 9 PM. I had to take an immediate decision. I prepared to go for the funeral, leaving my family in Botswana. My wife was capable of handling my business in my absence.

I attended the funeral. My little brother, Augustine, came with his little son, Ashish, and Irene came with their little son, Ruben, from Los Angeles. It was amazing that all nine children could come to pay our last respects to our mum. All our family members and friends attended the funeral.

On the day of the burial, it was raining heavily in Mumbai.

A bus was hired for the day. We reached the cemetery. It was not raining much initially, but at the time of the last prayer, rain came pouring down and the grave was flooded with water in minutes.

We had to wait for the rain to stop, but the monsoon rain in Mumbai does not stop. It pours continuously—sometimes, for two to three weeks. A couple of young boys jumped inside the grave and started pouring the water out. When we saw that it was almost empty, we lowered the coffin. The coffin was floating and we started covering the grave with sand. We decorated the grave with flowers. The rain was still pouring but we had to accept the situation.

Sometimes, we accept what the Lord wants to do for us. My mum had chest pain at night. Violet's daughter Regina was with her granny—my mum. She tried to comfort her by massaging her chest with pain balm. My dad phoned the doctor who was in Grant Road, which was about 10 miles from home. But it was heavily raining that night, so he took a long time to arrive. But before he arrived, my mum said to my dad and Regina, **"I am Holy now. Don't touch me."** My dad didn't dare touch her and looked at her, helplessly, passing away. The doctor arrived and declared that she was dead. My mum kept her devotions every day. She read the Bible in her spare time, prayed and fasted every Friday, and fasted for 40 days during the lent time. She was a good mother.

After mother's death, the Valsad house was completed. The Occupation Certificate was obtained. My dad asked me what name to give the house. I named it 'Flora'—my mother's name.

My dad was very happy about my good thought and named the house 'Flora.' The house was very big compared to the other houses in the area. The house became well known in Valsad—among our community. A year after completion of the house, my dad asked me to come with my family for the inauguration ceremony. I went to Valsad just to attend the ceremony. My dad handed over the keys of the house to me. He wanted my wife Priscilla to cut the ribbon and open the house. Our priest, Philemon Patel, and other priests from Mumbai prayed. Thereafter, my dad asked Priscilla to cut the ribbon and open the house. Priscilla denied saying that as *Pappa* was present there, she couldn't take the honor and that *Pappa* must have the honor. *Pappa* then cut the ribbon. Priscilla opened the main door of the house and garlanded my mum's photo, which was placed above the door. After Priscilla garlanded her photo, she declared that house was open with tears in her eyes. The house was built especially for my mother but Priscilla was given the honor in her place. We had a party with our church members and friends. Some of them even came from long distances.

The house was there but my mum was not there. My dad was alone in that house with two young servant girls, Manni and Savita. My mum had trained the two girls in household work and cooking, in Mumbai. They were so well-trained in cooking and taking care of the house that it became easy for my dad to be alone in Valsad. It was then that my dad got sick—it was his heart. There was no one to take care of him; I had to take care of him. I sent my wife with Augustine's sons, Amit and Ashish, to take care of dad.

My dad was very happy playing with seven-year-old Amit and four-year-old Ashish. But in Botswana, I had problems cooking and taking care of my children. I was struggling because I did not know to cook. In India, my wife took care of the house and lived with dad for 11 months. After that, my brother-in-law William Thomas retired from his work in Bhavnagar. My elder sister Freny and William came with their son Percy, to live with my dad. My wife returned to Botswana.

Thereafter, in a few years, my dad kept having cardiac problems and getting hospitalized. I had to travel again to see my dad. I went with my little daughter, Sylvia, to Valsad. We went to see dad in the hospital. He was in the municipality's hospital because there was no bed available in the private hospital for a cardiac patient. I was very unhappy about the place where he was kept in. I ordered to take him to a bigger city—Surat; it was our hometown, where my dad and I were born.

Surat was about 30 miles from Valsad. We could not get an ambulance on that day to transfer him to Surat's hospital. So, we hired a jeep and took him with a cylinder of oxygen attached to him. We reached the biggest hospital—Mahavir Hospital—that was the best in Surat in those days. He was put in a private room and a cardiologist took care of him. I stayed in Surat at Rosemary's house. We took good care of him, brought him back to Valsad and made him comfortable.

My dad always wanted to do something. So, when he started to move again with full strength, he told me that Simon uncle's son Ivor, who was with me in Botswana, should get married. He arranged a meeting with a family in Valsad for the marriage proposal.

Ivor was working in my company in Botswana. He had good standing and we were trying to get him married. The girl's father came to meet me and we had a good talk with him. My father was happy with the girl and her family. I agreed to it and the marriage was arranged. I returned to Botswana.

After that, in three months' time, my dad was admitted in the same municipal hospital in Valsad—but I was not informed.

Before going to the hospital, my dad had already bought the wedding saree (Indian apparel) for the girl, for the marriage. Ivor's father, my uncle Simon, died long before so my dad took up the responsibility of getting him married.

In Botswana, I prepared Ivor and sent him to get married. Ivor reached Bombay.

In Bombay, Ivor and his family were getting ready for the marriage. On the day before the marriage, the party left Bombay by train to arrive at the Valsad station. On arrival at the Valsad Station, people began entertaining the guests.

At that time, Nelson was with my dad. Dad was still in hospital on that day. Dad asked him to go get him a tender coconut for drinking. Nelson went to buy it. At that time, one of the hospital's nurses came and gave him an injection. The medication was not genuine and the nurse was an untrained person working at night. As soon as she gave him the injection, my dad died.

Nelson reached the bedside at that point, but he did not know what injection it was. The marriage party was at the Valsad station when dad died. Dad was very excited about the marriage but he could not attend it.

The marriage party was informed about the sudden death. The happiness turned into sadness and mourning. Ivor refused to get married at that point, but my brother, sisters and other family members convinced him that dad is still present and to get married without any celebration.

Ivor, with mixed feelings, was married in a simple ceremony. I was informed over the phone. I did not know that dad was in hospital. I was dreaming of and visualizing Ivor's marriage and celebrations at Valsad.

I reached Valsad the next day for the funeral. I met Ivor and his newly-wedded wife. They were both speechless. My dad was happy about Ivor because he was under my training and he was doing well. The day I arrived in Valsad, people were already waiting so we had to perform the burial ceremony of my father right away. They could not keep the body waiting for long because there was no mortuary in the city. They kept his body on a bed with lots of slabs of ice around him, as there were no funeral homes in the city. We had to obtain a municipality-issued certificate of death and bury the body at the Christian cemetery in Valsad on the same day as my arrival.

Dad's Last Words

He died when no one was at his bedside. But he left his last words on a stone slate, written with a chalk.

This was written to Rosemary (baby).

Language: Gujarati

Ishwar krupaye chinta karwano samay wahi gayo, Ishwar Mahan chhe, mane saru chhe, chinta karvi nahi, shantiye chhu.

Translation in English:

By the Grace of the Lord, the time of worries has passed. I am fine; don't worry about me. I am at peace.)

Both, my mum and dad were devout Christians and they left good words to give us peace after their departure. With faith, we know they are with the Lord in His heavenly Kingdom.

After the death of my dad, Freny, her husband William Thomas and son Percy occupied Flora house. The house was like a curse for the family. Freny built her own home near Flora and they shifted there. Flora was vacant.

My dad, when he was alive, gave the house—and all his belongings including mum's jewelry and his bank balance—to me, in his last will. Obviously, he knew that it was my money.

I had this understanding with dad: whatever is mine is yours and whatever is yours is mine because I am also yours. After getting all the jewelry, I distributed all the jewelry between my sisters and my older brother. My little brother did not get anything and I did not keep any of it for myself either. After my father's death, the honorable Pastor Philemon of Brethren church, Valsad helped me in transferring the house on my name. He knew all about our financial affairs because my dad shared details of our financial dealings in Africa with him.

I was in charge of the house. There was no one to take care of it. I visited occasionally, during my vacation time in December. We visited the house for only about three weeks. The first week we had to spend in cleaning the house. People broke the windowpanes and other things outside the house. They took fruits from the trees and made a mess in the yard. I had difficulties taking care of the house. I was there a couple times for my vacation, but I was never happy living there. The house was full of dust and sand inside, with lots of insects and an army of mosquitos. It was two weeks before we could live comfortably. But by the time we cleaned the house, it was time to return to Africa. But we felt like we visited our mother when I visited the house. My father's vision shattered. My mother visualized that we will never be happy in that house. She was exactly right.

My Mother

Flora Philip Hatia/Samuel

She was a mother that taught not only her children but also the people in the neighborhood and the community. She only had primary-level education but she could read and write very well and was wise. Behind the success of the Hatia family was my mother. She worked hard from the first day of her marriage. Village life is not easy. She lived with lots of hardships with the strict rules of my granny. My granny's living standards were like that of the Hindu culture. My mother had to accept certain unusual practices, which are not to be mentioned in this book. She started having children early in her life. She was married when she was 17 years old. She had 11 children. Two of them died at a young age. We were nine of us. When my dad moved to Bombay, she was still with my granny. Besides the household chores, she was helping my granny with her crochet work, making laces of metallic yarn.

When she moved to Bombay, she ruled herself. She started a small business from her house. There was a school in the neighborhood. She started vending roasted gram and peanuts at the front door of the house. Children started greeting her at the marketplace, calling her 'Chanewali' (gram vendor). One day, on the local train a boy introduced his mother and said: "Look! My 'Chanewali.' She was embarrassed and stopped the business. But she did not stop there.

She brought a herb called Bhangra, from Surat, and blended it into coconut oil to make hair oil. It was doing well. At that time, Irene was born. So, she called the hair oil's name as 'Irene Hair Oil.' The bottles were made and a label saying "Irene Hair Oil" was stuck on them. Then, it was sealed with a plastic top. I used to cover it with a seal.

The oil became popular in our neighborhood when my mum went to help a lady—the wife of our neighborhood grocery shop's owner. The lady was known as a madwoman; people used to be scared of passing by her door because they thought she had a demonic spirit. My mother took the oil and a bible with her. She sat by the lady and applied the oil on her hair. The lady was comforted and became very quiet. The husband was very thankful. The grocery owner bought the oil and started selling the oil in his shop. The news spread fast and the oil business was going well. But when my dad resigned from the Police office, the family faced a crunch. We stopped the business, as it needed capital to expand; we could not even meet ends at home. To feed nine children plus our uncle and aunt was getting harder and harder. What we went through in those days, I still think of—even today. It had a big impact on my mind. It made me a man in my childhood. Whatever happens to us is the plan of our Lord.

My mum started doing her old work of crochet lace, which I used to take right up to Pydhoni—a long journey by tram. I have mentioned this in my history previously.

My mother educated us to pray all the time. While going out of house, we had to pray and she'd keep watch. If we forgot, she'd remind us to pray. In the afternoon, when she had some quiet time, she used to take the Bible and read and pray. She rebuked us, loved us and trained us with house chores. Without her training, the family would be in chaos. Not only us but our uncles' families also got into the practice of evening devotion, every day before dinner. When mother died, the happiness of our family vanished.

"Poverty is a good teacher for future cautiousness and awareness. It becomes a charm of life because we live in such strong togetherness."

My Life in Mumbai

I was born between the first and the second world wars. At that time, the British government ruled India. The British Government was stringent in their laws and guidelines, but some British officers who were making adverse use of the laws, practiced brutality. Some of the officers were very compassionate and helped the general public. Some of them brought Christianity to India and developed Christian institutions to educate and provide medical needs to the general public regardless of colour, caste or creed.

1945, Bombay

I remember very clearly the day when I saw with my own eyes the brutality of British soldiers. I was about nine years old when I saw British soldiers marching in the street in front of our apartment. We used to live on the second floor in the middle portion of a building called Jilani Manzil—the building opposite the Portuguese Church in Dadar. The building still exists today.

It was wintertime; Bombay was a bit cool. It was about six o'clock in the evening when the British troops were marching and there was a curfew order. Usually, the city was very noisy but because of the curfew, the suburb was very quiet. The shops and houses were shut. My dad peeped at the marching soldiers from a small pigeonhole window above the main door. I climbed up in curiosity and peeped through a broken pane of the window. Inside the house, we kept silent because everyone was afraid of getting shot by the soldiers. The British soldiers managed to wreak havoc and create fear in the minds of the general public in Bombay. They used to shoot at sight if they saw anyone moving in the area during the curfew period.

I saw that suddenly, a shot was fired at our building. The soldier sat on his knee and took aim at our building. I thought they'd located us and that they were shooting at our window. I lost my grip on the iron bars of the window and fell down. My Dad was still looking at the scene. Suddenly, we heard the cry of a big man, saying "*Maa, Maa*". We were the only Guajarati family in that area. In the Gujarati language, "*Maa*" means mother. Our neighbor thought that it was the cry of my uncle, Wilson. He was the only one in our area who used to call his mother '*Maa*.'

Soon after, when the British troop passed by, the time of curfew was over and the British soldiers cleared the area. We rushed out of the house to see who was crying and calling out to their mother. We saw a young man wounded on the street just below our apartment. He was shot near our apartment door, on the second floor, and had fallen down onto the street from there. The British people did not care about him and walked away. The man was a freedom fighter—an angry, young Muslim man that threw a brick at the passing British troop and accepted death for it.

The man was in agony. People gathered there to help him in getting treatment from a doctor. But it was too late; he was shot above his chest and his head was full of blood because he had fallen from the second floor. The guy was bleeding very badly. We saw him looking at us helplessly. Some people were comforting him by giving him first aid but he died in front of our eyes shortly before the ambulance arrived. The general public seemed very angry but the British soldiers were so strict that they would not allow long queues under any circumstances.

In Bombay, we had queues for kerosene fuel for stoves. Standing in long queues at government grain-shops, under the hot sun, was our life.

People were issued rationing cards. Those rationing cards still exist in India for getting cheap food as well as an identity card. The milk-bottle kiosk lines were another example of people standing in long lines to get their daily needs.

British officers used to shoot women, children and the elderly mercilessly if the curfew time had started and the innocent people were not aware of it. Such brutalities were intolerable. We lived in fear at all times. I was in the 4th grade when India became independent. We were given paper flags and a box of sweets (*mithai*) in our hands. After the flag-hoisting ceremony, we sang patriotic songs before getting sweets and then with much cheer and joy, we dispersed. To be honest, I did not know what was going on but I was thrilled upon receiving the sweets on that auspicious day. I could not resist eating the sweets, but I did not want to open the box. So, I handed it over to my mum. On the way home, I opened the box from the bottom and took some sweets. At home, when I handed the box over to my mum, I thought that she would not know that I'd taken some sweets. When she opened the box, she laughed and said: "Oh! Some rat has been eating sweets from the bottom of the box." I was embarrassed and looked down. Mum patted me and gave me one piece of the sweet in my hand and smiled at me. Those good old days are memoirs of my innocence.

The Village's Herbal Vayed (Village Doctor) from Maharashtra

There was an illiterate couple from a village in Maharashtra but they were village doctors with knowledge of herbal medicines. They used to treat people and give herbal medication without charging any money. The man's name was Shanker and his wife's name was Muktabai.

They were of the Mangarudi (Maharashtrian tribe) tribe. They often visited our home, checked our pulse and gave us medication. They were good people so my mum used to entertain them and offer them food and tea. She spoke to Muktabai and gave her time to relax at our house because they usually travelled long distances.

Muktabai became good friends with our family. They gave us herbal medication but they did not ask for money. If we offered them money for the medication, they'd refuse to take it. They used to say that it was God's gift and that they did not sell. But my mum used to give her money as a gift and she used to take that.

Shanker, however, used to stutter. He came home to give treatment to my dad. My dad asked him if he could cure his hemorrhoids. He said that he could do that by performing a small surgery to extract all the hemorrhoids. My dad asked him which hospital he'd have to go to for the procedure. He said that he could perform it on dad's worktable itself, at the Police office. My dad asked if he was going to give him any anesthesia. He said no and that he will use his techniques and that my dad will not have any cut or pains. My dad was still taking his words as a joke but Shanker was serious.

On one Saturday, Shanker came to do the surgery. My dad lay on a bed and they closed the door of the room. Shanker performed the surgery. After about an hour, Shanker opened the door and we saw that he had filled two huge bottles, shaped like pineapples, with blood. We were surprised to see that my dad, however, was completely relieved. Shanker gave him a ring made out of tortoiseshell and told my dad to never remove it from his finger, as it would stop the hemorrhoids from relapsing.

Shanker did not ask for money for the surgery. My dad offered him 50 rupees but he refused to take it. My mum then gave some money to Muktabai as a gift.

Believe me or not—one day, in Africa, my dad was searching for something in his suitcase. I asked him what he was looking for. He said he was searching for that ring which he had taken off as he thought it looked very ugly and was very old. My dad had hemorrhoid pains again. He found the ring and immediately put it on his finger but it did not work. The magic of the ring was gone. My dad suffered after that. He went to see the doctor and took ointments for hemorrhoids.

I Lived in the Olden Days

We used stone slates with stone pens in primary school. In high school, we used black, blue or red ink with a nib on a holder and fountain pens. Ball pens were not known to us.

When the radio was invented, we used to visit shops and see how the voice came from the box. It was the best entertainment—all over India. My mum and I went to a shop called Opera house Radio shop in Mumbai and bought a 'Mullard' brand, German-made radio for 300 rupees—which was like $30,000 for us, in those days.

A technician connected the radio. He ran the antenna above the roof area of our apartment and connected a long wire to our water tap. The radio was an excellent source of entertainment for our neighbors and us because they used to come and share the happiness.

After that came the transistors and the record players with big spools. Then came the car radio and the tape recorder—which were amazing inventions. Then came the multi-cassette recorder players played in cars and on jukeboxes at restaurants. And now, there are digital players.

Then came the black-and-white televisions, then color televisions and now, the digital ones. Hardly anyone had this instrument in our area, in India. But we used to see it displayed in glass windows of shops. If any neighborhood house got a television, the owner would invite certain friends to come over and enjoy the shows. Many people used to peep through the windows.

Then came the computers, cell phones and many more things. Invention does not stop. The rockets and people walking on the moon and satellites are crowding the sky but people cannot live without them.

The modern digital televisions, cell phones and many other gadgets work with the help of satellites. It is a new world getting new inventions—which I cannot catch up with. Life is moving faster and faster. The Bible is proving to be true and events denoting the signs of times are now showing frequency. The day of the Lord is getting nearer.

My Early Life in Bombay

My primary school education was done at a municipality school in the Agar Bazaar area, near Prabhadevi in Mumbai—a free-of-cost school. For my secondary school, I went to a private school in the Matunga suburb, Mumbai, about 3 miles away from my house.

King George High was located near Dr. Ambedker's bungalow. Dr. Ambedker is the chief architect of the Constitution of India. He was from an untouchable caste—a caste many upper-caste Hindus would not touch or come near, but he became a nobleman and drafted the constitution of India which has given good shape to the democratic government of India.

In my school, all the students were Hindus. I was the only non-Hindu but at that time, there was no religious segregation like in modern days of the 21st century.

I had three good, prominent friends. One was Mr. Vijay Manjreker; a well-known cricketer who studied in my school. He was such a cricket-crazy boy that on the day of our high school final examination, he left the examination to play cricket on Ram Narayan Ruia-Podar College's cricket ground. He expected failure in school, but he came out to become a player of India-Eleven and became well-known all over the cricketing world.

The second prominent person was Bal Thakre, whom I met at a gym called Amar Hind Mandal of Dadar, Mumbai. I was the only good friend he had. He used to be an expert in Hu-Tu-Tu (a sport) and Langadi game and I was an expert in Kho-Kho (an Indian game). One day, when I was selected to play a match on a national playground with other Mumbai teams, Bal Thakre was not chosen because his weight was over 100 lbs. He fasted for three days, brought his weight down to 98 lbs and got himself selected for the match. He was the only one that used to shout my name with joy from the place where he was sitting during my Kho-Kho games, and I used to call out his name when he played Hu-Tu-Tu and Langadi. He was good at both these games because he was a tall and strong man.

When my departure to Africa was confirmed, Bal Thakre took me to an Iranian restaurant in front of a Portuguese church in Dadar and we had tea together. He had money and I did not have money even to buy tea. He was 9 years older than me. In a few years' time, I heard that he had become a party's leader and had good name and fame in India—and universally.

The third was a small boy called Anil Mohile who became a musician—a very famous one—in India.

As we grew up, our needs grew, too. But money was short. My travels to Pydhoni were tiring on the slow tram-ride of about three hours. I used to hand over the lace my mother made to a businessman, who in return gave 15 rupees (21 cents today) and more yarn for more work. The travel was tedious. I used to sit in the tram for hours. After handing over the lace to the businessman, I used to return with the yarn and hard-earned money—that was another risk for me. I used to put my money in my pant pocket and hold it with one hand because I was afraid I might lose it or someone would steal it from me. I had to struggle because the shortages at home made me take risks.

In India, most people drink tea. My mum was particular about her favourite brand: 'The Orange Pekoe.' I had to take bus route number "F" and reach Tardev Bridge. Near the bridge, there was a Parsi man's shop. I used to buy tea from him every other month. Now, 'The Orange Pekoe' tea is seen in American shops. 'Brook Bond' was the brand. In my house, I used to be the runner for buying grocery because my sisters could not go out and my brothers were either too big or too small.

My Education

I passed my high school examination but failed in the state exam. I had a chance to appear for two subject papers in May 1955, but the Lord had another plan for me. When I reached Ndola, Central Africa, there was no school for me. In Bombay, I was dreaming about big colleges in the foreign country because I saw in movies that all the big colleges where all the foreign students were freely moving about for their studies were abroad. The colleges had gardens around the campus. I found a night class. I started going to school with all adults studying with me. My mathematics and science subjects were of a higher level than theirs. They were doing elementary math. I stopped going to the school. In Zambia, I started my correspondence college education. I took bookkeeping and accountancy. I was getting a good grip on my studies. I passed my Intermediate certificate in Accountancy. I joined college for a degree course. I took the ACCA course offered by a college in London. I did the course so I could gain knowledge for my business. I failed in Roman laws. Actual, practical accountancy knowledge was good enough for me. I did not need the certificate. I was given a "Fellow" degree by the London College. My degree was certified by the FIAB (Fellow of International Association of Bookkeepers) and FBSC (Fellow of British Society of Commerce.). I did not need the signing authority but it helped me when I registered my companies. I was the public officer of my companies, so I could sign papers. I taught many young girls and boys. They used to keep records of accounts for me. I have good knowledge but it was of no use in America because the bookkeeping was done on computers and they had a software called Quick-book. Accountancy became simple. Nevertheless, I still had good practical knowledge of accountancy.

My Life Plan by God

My father was in Northern Rhodesia, Central Africa. There, the immigration law was that children under 16 could get permits to join their parents. I was already 16 so, obviously, I could not get the permit. But just for me, I believe, the law changed from 16 to 18 years of age. I fit in with that new amendment. My dad immediately planned to take me to Africa, because he was lonely.

Dad wanted me to go to Africa. He wrote to my mum to get me ready with some new clothes and other travelling items. He applied for my permanent visa to go to Northern Rhodesia (now Zambia). My mum bought suiting material. The suit was custom-made by "Ferns Tailor" who had their shop in our complex. It was my first suit. She bought shirting material and had my shirts custom-tailored by "Lobo Tailor." We bought rainproof bedding cover and a comforter, some sheets, pillows and one necktie along with three pairs of socks.

In India, in our school days, we did not wear socks because it was humid and hot. We used to wear sandals because it was scorching in Bombay in all seasons. Inside the bedding, there were some pockets where she kept some 'Amrutanjan Pain Balm' bottles—because there was no other painkiller—and some snacks and cookies. My maternal uncle, Walter-*mama,* brought the famous butter biscuits and Nankhatai (sweet biscuits) from Surat. I had some spicy snacks, too. I was getting excited about getting lots of gifts and new clothing.

My tickets came through Cox and Kings. Our church treasurer, Jonathan Roberts, was in charge of the office. He brought the tickets to us. My dad sent 30 Sterling pounds through the company. Jonathan uncle arranged traveller's checks for me. My passport was a bit of a problem. My name was Alexander Hatia but I wanted the name Samuel because my dad had sent tickets for Alexander Samuel. I went to the Police Commissioner's office—my dad's ex-office—for assistance. I met Anny Fernandez, who came with me to the magistrate office and changed my name from Hatia to Samuel. My dad helped

Anny Fernandez in getting a job at the Police Commissioner's office. The Fernandez family was our neighbor when we lived in their building. Anny's mother used to visit us often. Her brother Georgie and sister Rosemary were our close friends. I remember attending Rosemary's marriage.

My elder sister Freny and my aunt Santosh-*masi*, (mother's sister) both worked and they were earning very little. They both contributed 12.50 rupees (18 cents today) each and bought one "Brownie" Kodak camera for me with two rolls of film. It was a very precious item for me. I took care of it because that was my first camera. I did not know how to take photos. I had to learn loading the film and clicking the camera.

On the day of my departure, Mum woke up very early in the morning. She wanted to buy more milk from the milkman who came at 4.30 AM. I used to get up many times to get cream balls from the milkman. Violet and I used to have quarrels about getting the cream ball, which was given as a gift by the milkman. Early in the morning, water came only for one hour. Water was rationed in Bombay. Mum filled water containers daily. We expected many guests and visitors to come to our house to wish me farewell. Water was in shortage and even more so in Mumbai because the population was escalating daily. We used to store two drums of water—of 45 gallons each—daily. Our close relatives came two days earlier. The day before my departure, I took photos of my family members with my camera. Some of the photos are still with me, as remembrances of the day.

My mum made special breakfast for me. She knew what I liked. She made 'Sweet Sev' (vermicelli) and fried egg and gave it to me with roti (Indian bread). She was very busy that day. In the evening, the family brought fresh flower garlands. I was getting confused. I was not happy as the departure hour was nearing. In the beginning, I was excited because I was getting lots of gifts. But the thoughts of departure made me unhappy soon.

My Voyage to Africa

On the drizzly morning of August 8, 1955, I departed India from Bombay Port Trust, Bombay, leaving behind my beloved mum, brothers, sisters and relatives. I was naïve and ignorant of where I was heading. I suppose Abraham had the same feelings. Abraham traveled through a desert on dry sand and I traveled on water, on a huge ship named SS. Karanja—a British-India Company steamer shuttle between East Africa and India. I boarded the ship after passing through the immigration and customs formalities and climbed the stairs between the dock and the ship. I did not look back because I was in agony of leaving my mum and family. I looked down; I was crying internally but I showed bravery to my mum because she was in tears.

I can imagine what Abraham must have gone through when he was called upon by the Lord to leave home and his loved ones.

I was a third-class passenger; there was no one to guide me as to where I should look for my bunk. I went searching for my bunk and came across many passengers. The bunk was at the bow-end of the ship. It was under the stairs going to the upper deck. I established my baggage and rushed on the middle-deck towards the area where my family was standing. I stood there, staring at my mum and family. Mum was wiping her eyes with a handkerchief. Occasionally, she waved at me. At about 3 PM, the ship started moving. I started waving at my family faster and in turn, they also waved. I realized that I was on my own. As the ship took distance from the dock, I kept waving but I could no longer see them. When I saw the Gateway of India, it was just a black dot. I sauntered to my bunk. I lay on the bedding and remained on it for a long time.

The ship was sailing and I was alone, not knowing what to do. I sat on the bunk, still wiping my tears and keeping my head on my pillow. This may be the agony Joseph felt when he was sold to go to Africa. Why did the Lord call me to go to Africa? Why me? I did not know. Late in the evening, I had heavy head and I started vomiting. I had to walk to a gutter-like drainage. I threw up and became very nauseous; I must have done that about three times. Then, I sat on my bed for a while. After a little while, a man came to me with *Ganthoda* (Indian spice—like dry horseradish) powder and told me to put it on my tongue and drink some water. It was very spicy stuff. I'd never had such medication but it worked.

I was feeling fine. I did not know that I had seasickness. I never traveled on water before—not even on a small boat. This was my first experience. I was crying; I had a headache and I was hungry because I had not eaten the whole day. At about 6 PM, there was bell-ringing that meant that the canteen was open and food was being served but I was not in a mood to eat. The evening was scary for me; I was afraid of being alone and I was hungry. But as I started throwing up, I could not go and eat at the canteen. The money was paid but in a situation like this, I did not have the courage to move from my bed. At seven o'clock, my mind was diverted. I started visualizing my brothers and sisters gathered with my mum, sitting in circle. They were singing hymns, reading the Bible and praying. This was our daily routine. Without this devotion time, we would not get even the evening's meal. On the first night, I had a series of dreams of my home and I had many experiences. Everyone around my bunk area was sad. They were all grown-ups and they were with their family. I looked around to see if anyone would come to me to comfort me but no one came. The second morning, when I was starving, I opened the snacks. I started eating and thinking about my mum and what she must be doing. I could not sleep at night because water kept getting sprayed on me from the stairs, which was near my bed. I was a third-class passenger and I had to accept the situation. I could not complain to anyone. It happened because the ship picked up speed at night. My bunk was right at the bow of the ship. As the ship went up, I got sprayed. I was sleeping on what felt like a seesaw. I covered myself with my blanket and tried to take a nap.

On the third morning, at about 4 AM, the ship stopped. I was feeling good. I climbed the stairs near my bed and saw that in front of the ship; there were lots of lights. It was some port. The ship was anchored in the middle of the sea. At about 6 AM, the ship started moving towards the port. The natural beauty of the morning and the ship sailing towards the land was indescribable. I was sitting on the top deck, watching the beauty of the multiple colors of the clouds changing by the minute, birds singing, the sun rising and the cool wind blowing. I felt intoxicated by the atmosphere surrounding me. If the world's beauty was so amazing, how much more beautiful would heaven be, I wondered. I was not sick anymore.

The port was that of Karachi, Pakistan. When the ship docked at the port, I realized that I was hungry and thirsty. I went to the canteen for my first meal on the ship. I had not eaten a solid meal for two days. I was snacking all the time and drank water from the water dispenser nearby. I had a good, hearty breakfast that morning. After that. I was not sick anymore. I had not had a bath for two days. So, I decided to take a shower—which was on the top deck. I opened the tap and started showering but, to my surprise, the water was salty. I was a third-class passenger, so I thought that that was the facility given to us. But after my shower, I came out and met a man standing there. I smiled at him and he looked at me and said that the water was salty. I nodded affirmatively. He told me that after that saltwater shower, I had to get into another shower for sweet water—which only ran for a few minutes. I went in and quickly washed the saltwater from my head to toe. It was my first experience. The following day onwards, I used to get up early and bathe with saltwater and then get into the other shower for a wash-up with sweet water. After my bath, I read the Bible and prayed every morning. At 7 AM, the breakfast bell rang. I used to be very regular for my breakfast, sitting at the same seat every day.

At Karachi port, I had good experiences. The ship was busy loading cargo and many laborers were doing physical work. I saw a vendor selling some fruits. I bought a green pear from the vendor by lowering a basket with a rope; I spent one Indian Rupee on it. I was eating this fruit for the first time. It was a sweet and juicy fruit. I'd never had this kind fruit before. I was wondering what kind of fruit it was. I thought that it was some kind of apple. Now, every time I eat a pear, I get the memory of my day at the Karachi port. This happens to me every now and then. When I walk past fruit sections and see those green pears, the Karachi port's visuals comes alive in my mind.

On that day, some young girls and boys came with a gramophone-like player and played music. I joined them and we became friends. They were born in Africa to Indian parents. I had good company; they were experienced voyagers and I was not one.

The ship was loading rice the whole night. We stayed on the ship that day and that night. The next day, at about 10 AM, we left Karachi for Africa. That journey, going from port to port, was like Paul's experience on his sea journey. On the fifth day, when the ship was traveling through the sea of Suqutra (Socotra), we faced a big storm. The ship was moving side to side, and the sea was very rough. I was scared; I was on my bunk praying for saving ourselves from the storm. Because of the spraying of the water and the ship making all sorts of noises, I could not sleep that scary night—but Christ was by my side. He gave me peace and strength. The next day, a sailor met me on the deck and told me that such storms were normal. It happened every time they traveled through the sea of Socotra. The sailor was a very good man. He asked me where I was from. I told him that I was born in Surat and lived in Bombay. He said that he was also from Surat—a place called Aulpad near Rander. I told him about my grandma's family in Rander. The sailor was from the same village as my grandma. I gave him my family name and he said that they lived in his neighborhood. He took me to his cabin and gave me good food: fish curry and rice—just like home. He gave me his hammock to sleep in and Indian music to listen to. I was no longer worried about the sea. God provided me with more strength and facilities on my voyage. I was not alone; God was with me. I met other young boys and girls and we became friends. We made a gang and explored the ship from bow to stern. I used to read my Bible and say my prayers every morning and evening and fasted on Fridays. Fasting was my mum's teaching. It was a painful practice at home when I was with my mum. But in the absence of my mum, I have kept up the practice to this day. On the 15th of August, we had Indian Independence day celebrations. The Captain had a flag-hoisting ceremony and we were given exotic food with lots of sweets. I really enjoyed the food on that day.

The ship arrived at the Zanzibar port of East Africa in the morning. It was anchored in the middle of the sea because there was no port at Zanzibar at that time. We disembarked through a small side door onto a ferry, which was made up of about four oil drums tied to a wooden plank. We reached the port after 12 days of travel. It was a wonderful feeling to be on land. I was a stranger and did not know where to go, but God is good—I went with my ship companion and He provided me an Indian gentleman, a schoolteacher, who usually came to the port to see people coming from his country. He greeted us in our language and told us to go to his house with him. He took us to his house and there, his wife prepared a cup of tea and gave us varieties of Indian snacks. The man was so kind and nice that he took us walking and showed us the whole island. The island was small. The roads were so narrow that you could touch both the sidewalls when walking. The island had a strong smell of coconuts and cloves–the commodities that were the main exports of the island. We went to see other Indian families and some good buildings on the island. My eyes were searching for a church but I could see only mosques, Arab-named schools and a cinema theater. The Arabs previously ruled the island so the island was established with the religion of Islam only.

The same evening, we embarked the ship and sailed for the next port.

The day after, we arrived at the Mombasa port. The beauty of the view of the ship scrolling past Mombasa was much more beautiful than that of Karachi port's. My bed was under the stairs, so I used to go up and down frequently. When the ship docked at the port, I saw a line of soldiers of the British-African Army. I was confused to see a line of soldiers standing on the dock. The soldiers were nicely dressed in khaki uniforms. But amazingly, I noticed that all the soldiers looked alike. I looked hard to spot any difference in their faces but they all looked similar to me. I was seeing Africans for the first time. I was confused and wondering how they differentiated one man from the other. I was wrong. One of the local Indian men told me that there were lots of differences in their faces but since I was seeing them for the first time, I was unable to make out. I was supposed to be at Mombasa for three days. My mother's cousin Lavinya-*masi*, whom I wrote about earlier, lived there and I expected her to be picking me up but she was not to be seen. I waited at the port till about 11.30 AM but nobody came. Fortunately, a ship-friend's relative took me. He had a bicycle shop. I was given a room—a fantastic accommodation with a beautiful bed and clean sheets. He was a busy man so he did not have time during the day but in the evenings, he took us to show us around Mombasa city. This I cannot forget to write about—the food given to me was also fantastic. They were a Hindu family but they did not have any problems with my belief. God was with me there, too. I did not have any problems for three days. I walked in the city during the daytime and looked at the foreign shops. They were very different from those in Bombay; the whole environment was different. I thought that I would be left alone at the port but God provided me with more than what I expected there. I had a chance to write to my mum from the Mombasa post office. I bought an airmail paper and started writing to my mum, with lots of tears, about my journey. I managed to mail my letter.

After three days of a good vacation in the Mombasa city, we boarded the ship for our onward journey. It was a three-day voyage on the ship, with lots of excitement, good friends and good food provided by the ship's canteen.

We reached Dar-Es'-Salaam, another Arabian-dominated city. I found many Indians in East Africa and found some Christians, too. The Christians I met were Anglicans. Most of them were either Catholic or Anglican, but the name of Jesus was well-known in the city. I did not have much time with them but I was happy to find Christians among the Hindus and the Islamic majority of the Aga Khan sect.

After three days of touring of Dar-Es'-Salaam, I boarded a private truck to travel towards Northern Rhodesia (now Zambia). We were seven of us on the truck. There were wooden benches provided for travelers. It was about 11 AM on Thursday when we started our journey. We traveled through the jungles of Tanganyika (now Tanzania). The month of August was usually cold in Tanzania. It was extremely cold at night. I had no jersey so I took my suit's jacket and pulled it around myself but I was freezing. I kept my eyes closed and looked down, pulling my jacket closer and trying to keep warm.

The truck driver saw that I was the only young one among the older crowd and became friends with me. We stopped at Dodoma, a small town where we had dinner at about 8 PM. The city was mostly dominated by Gujarati-speaking people. We had Indian restaurants and exotic food. That was on Thursday night. We traveled onwards at night, through the jungle. I used to peep through the front window of the canopy. Every time any animal was seen by the driver, he alerted me to look at the wildlife. We traveled throughout the night and the next day, at about 11 AM, we reached a small village called Irringa. There, we met some Indians. They arranged for lunch—fried spiced potatoes and *purees* (fried roti), rice and dal—which was very satisfying.

Amazing Grace

I believe that most of the Lord's blessings were showered on me throughout my life in Africa—in return for that one day's fast and prayer. Despite my hunger and the long journeys, I fasted as my mum taught me to and received God's grace.

We were all hungry because of the long journey, but because it was Friday, I was fasting. I did not eat on that day. I walked around the shopping area of the village. At about 12 in the noon, we started our journey. In the east African jungle, I saw many wild animals, which fascinated me. I had seen those animals in books but there, I saw them alive—in front of me. Coming from the hot weather of Bombay to the cold of the Tanzanian jungle, for me, was extreme. After a 12-hour journey, we reached Mbeya, a small town near the border of Northern Rhodesia (now Zambia). The truck was parked by the roadside at 12.30 AM. The place was mountainous so it was colder than in the moving truck. I was holding the jacket but it was of no use. I was shivering in the bitter cold and hungry, too. In the morning, at about 4 AM, a man approached the truck and spoke in Gujarati—my language. He asked me to get down and go with him to his house. The truck was standing by the gate of his house. He heard our noise and came to invite us to his home. For me, he was a God-sent angel. He was from the Ismailia Khoja—a Muslim sect. He prepared a fireplace inside the house, with a homemade heater and burning coal. The coal-burning heater was called, in the local language, a 'Baura.' Whatever it was called, it gave good heat and made me very comfortable. God is great; the family made hot tea and hot *purees* (fried rotis are called *purees* in India). It was like the Manna, given to me by the Lord in the wilderness of East Africa. I prayed and ate and broke my fast in the morning, in Mbeya. Let me quote that at that particular time, I felt the Lord's blessings on me. He was with me and I did not know. I think he accepted my fasting and prayer. God was in the wilderness of Tanzania, too.

The next day, there was lovely sunshine, though it was wintertime. I could walk with my jacket in the city. The jacket was the only blessing from my mum. She told me that I must wear the suit to church in the foreign country. In India, we do not use coats because of the severe heat. I had never experienced cold like I did in Tanzania. The Saturday morning was pleasant in Mbeya. We were boarding at India clubhouse. It was the cheapest accommodation in town. The hilly town with Swahili-speaking people had some Indian businessmen as well. I was very comfortable; I walked into the town and met many young Indian boys and girls. They came to the club for sports and for social gatherings at the club. I think it was the only place of entertainment for Indians. I was happy meeting them. The next day was Sunday. I was craving to go to the church. So, I walked towards a church, but did not have the courage to enter the church because I saw tall African men and women; they were strangers to me. I stood on the road to see what kind of church it was. I heard the hymn that they were singing; it had a nice English-like rhythm to it but was in the Swahili language. After the singing was over, I heard the man speaking—maybe, it was the sermon. I walked off but felt good in my heart that at least I attended church. I was happy but somehow, I was not very satisfied because I did not enter the church. Anyway, God gave me comfort because I heard the hymns. I walked the whole town, over and over again. The third day, a man came looking for me and said to me that my dad was his friend and he'd paid for my bus ticket to travel to Zambia. He was a Muslim-man—a very jolly character. He took me to his office-cum-house and gave me good food to eat. He told me that we would be traveling the next day. All seven of us were going to Zambia. I was given special preference and a special seat on the bus. At times, I sat by the driver to see the jungle and the animals. God was with me there, too, because I was given special treatment.

We reached the Tanzania-Zambia border at about 11 AM. I was not scared at all because the bus belonged to my dad's friend named Lal Miyan of Sheikh transport. We completed all the paperwork and went on the journey towards my destination—Ndola city of Zambia. It was noontime when we reached Tunduma (Tanzania) and crossed into the Zambian side of the border, at Nkonde. After passing through the formalities at the borders, we started our journey towards Isoka (meaning, a big snake), a bigger village near the border in Zambia. There, we met the family of a Muslim businessman; they entertained us. After lunch, we went on our journey through the jungle but there were not many animals in the jungle. We passed by many small villages. One of the villages was Chisoka (meaning, small snake). At about 4 AM, we reached a place called Kapirimposhi. It was cold in the Zambian town.

There, we met a certain Gujarati family who entertained us with the 'Baura' fire lighted and a hot cup of tea with some Indian snacks. We really enjoyed the hospitality. We left the town and went on our journey but at about 7 AM, the bus stopped because the engine was emitting smoke. It had a major breakdown. The local citizens did not have any problems. They had lived the jungle life all their lives; they cooked their meal by the roadside and waited for the bus to start.

They did not mind waiting for the whole day. A message was sent and the mechanic was supposed to come. Ndola was about 30 miles from the breakdown area. One of the persons from our group took a ride with some passer-by, in his car. He returned with an open van and took us to Ndola.

I was sitting at a friend's home with a crowd of Guajarati people. My dad came in at about 5 PM after his duty. He was looking around for me and asked the people if his son had arrived or not. I stood up and walked to him. He was surprised to see that I was so big! He hugged me and he had a smile on his face for the rest of the day.

I met my dad and I started my new life in Africa.

My Life in Africa: Rhodesia

1955/Ndola, Northern Rhodesia (Zambia)

I was with my dad but I felt lonely because he worked the whole day in his office and I had nothing to do. I was missing my fast life in Mumbai, now that I had landed in the slow pace of a third-world country. It was almost one month since I'd left India. I asked my dad, on a Saturday, that I wanted to go to a hair-cutting salon. He smiled and took me walking to a friend's clothing shop. Behind the shop was his house. We went to the house and had some tea with him. After that, the friend, Kassam, took me to his backyard and offered me a wooden stool and covered me with a cloth and started cutting my hair. I was embarrassed because I had never had a haircut in the open. Anyway, it was an experience that I cannot forget. The small city was cute and charming but did not have a hairdressing salon for non-whites. That was my first experience of color discrimination—the terrible law of the land. I could not understand why we were discriminated against. One day, I wanted to drink soda as dad and I were passing by a restaurant. My dad went and bought a bottle of Coca-Cola and we shared the drink standing on the road. I was accustomed to going inside the restaurant and sitting and drinking. But there, too, non-whites were not allowed to sit. I was not very happy but I drank and returned the bottle to get the 5 cents back, which was taken as a deposit.

My feeling was:

"For blacks, we were too white and for whites, we were too black". That is called color discrimination.

On Sunday, we went to a church dominated by Europeans but there was no discrimination. I asked my dad about it and he told me that the law was not effective in the church. There, people were so kind and friendly that I felt very comfortable. Very soon, I joined a youth group. I could not speak good English because English was only my second language. Plus, my pronunciations and my Indian accent were very different. Many times, I could not understand what my friends were saying. I had a tough time, but there were a couple of girls and boys who were very kind to me. They helped me settle in nicely in the church group. I used to attend the group regularly, which helped me communicate with them. For learning English, I used to listen to the BBC news channel to get the pronunciations right and to get some style in my speech. At the youth group, I was regular not only to have Bible discussions but also because I was getting some spoken-English practice. My first birthday, December 14, 1955, in Africa was not celebrated. No one cared about my birthday. I was sitting and listening to the radio, which said that a lady in the USA, Rosa Parks, was in jail because she refused to give up her seat on the bus to a white person. I did not know if Rosa Parks was black or white. It was disturbing news that just for a bus seat a person could be in jail. I was not in the mood because it was my birthday and I was dreaming about my mum, my family and the food she usually made for my breakfast. It was a small and cheap celebration but it was the memory of my mum's love that made me sad.

The Lord's Blessing for Me

My job in Northern Rhodesia

I was employed without pay in a retail shop to learn the local language and to learn business in one months' time. The owner was delighted because I became good help to the shopkeeper. The shop's owner was Maganbhai Naik of M. Naik and Company—a good gentleman with a smart personality. Always dressed well and though not very educated, he spoke English very well. He had a lot of business experience. He was a good teacher for me. He would not allow me to read newspapers or books in the shop. He disciplined me well; he wanted me to concentrate on business only. When there were no customers, we had to arrange all the items in the shop in order. We always kept the shop clean and attended customers like friends. I lived with him at his house, in the beginning. His wife was the best cook and a hard-working woman. If I do not mention them in my history, I would feel guilty.

Maganbhai Naik and his good-natured wife were my inspirations and helped throughout my life.

In three months' time, my dad opened an Indian grocery business with a partner named Manubhai Patel. He had good experience in the field of grocery business. I was naive and had no experience in selling Indian commodities. The name of the business was very funny—'Luxmundi'. In the Arabic language, it meant 'The Light of the World.' Everyone felt that it was a funny name, but the main point was that it was known as an Indian grocery. I was in charge of the place and started my life selling all kinds of Indian grocery items. Most of the buyers were Indians and I was very comfortable with them. I was doing well and ran the business in good profits but the partner was not very happy; he wanted to siphon money and pocket it.

One day, he came to me and asked me to pack most of the grocery—which I did. He filled in railway dispatch forms with receiver's name, a grocery shop in Lusaka and asked me to sign the railway dispatch documents and the delivery slip. I refused to do anything like that. I did not allow him to take the grocery from the shop. I asked him to wait till my dad got there. He was furious and went away. In the evening, my dad came to the shop and I showed him the packed boxes. My dad called the partner, Manaubhai Patel, to ask for an explanation. He was speechless. Then, he said that he was not interested in the business and asked us to wind up and sell the goods to the Indian grocery in Lusaka, the capital city of Zambia.

I was not mature enough to take over; neither was my dad. Because he was working for a company under a contract, we had to give it up and sell our business. In this, my dad lost some money but it was not a big deal.

The Shopkeeper job: A blessing

My dad then arranged for a job for me in an Indian shop, as a salesman. I worked there very sincerely and all my wages went straight to my dad. I lived at the house of the shop's owner. I lived there like their family member. They were of the Hindu faith and initially, they invited me to the rituals that they performed and to sing along with them the Gujarati devotional songs, but I respectfully declined. I did not attend any of that but I regularly read my bible and said my prayers—every morning.

They honored that and they were impressed by my faith and my faithfulness at work. I was paid British Sterling Pounds 17.50 per month. I did not get my wages as it went straight to my dad. Our money was sent to Bombay to take care of the huge family. The educational and other expenses of my brothers and sisters were important and we worked hard to provide for them their day-to-day needs. The family with whom I lived was pure vegetarian and I lived the same way with them. The food was excellent. I lived like it was my own house and the owner's wife taught me lots of housework and how to behave in the house. The Lord provided for all my needs—a good family, good food and good work. My dad and I never missed out on going to our church at any cost. The only problem was that on Christmas or other festivals, I was sad because there was no celebration of my festivals at the house where I lived. After church service, dad went to his house without saying anything and I went to my house without uttering a word because we were both sad. When we attended church on festivals, we used to enjoy every bit of the church service and used to sing loudly. But after all that, returning home made us sad. Imagine finding food like *Vaal*-beans and bread on the table on festival days!

That job in Ndola was perfect. Though it was not very rewarding, the owner, Karsondas and his wife, Godavaryben were very kind, old people. Work was mainly in the shop but living with the family, I always volunteered to help the mother whenever I could; after all, Jesus taught us servanthood. I call her my second mother. She kept me like she did her own sons. In the neighborhood, people thought I was their son and had returned from my school in India. I was very happy with them but everything—good and bad—comes to an end and I found a job in Luanshya town; it was one with more challenges.

Work with Training and Skills

My dad found me the job in Luanshya town, which was about 25 miles from Ndola.

I found it to be a challenging job but it was hard work in return for more money. The family environment there was not so good but there, too, I offered my hand and worked at home. This helped me as they started looking at me favorably. Though I worked from morning till night; I was kept occupied even on weekends.

The family whom I lived with was the owner of the three shops. I lived with them along with three other employees. I worked there for about seven months. At that job, I learnt to build a complete bicycle. I was given this extra job on Saturday afternoons so that I did not escape to visit my family and friends—or go to the movies. I was not interested in doing all that; I was more interested in learning more of such skilled work. If not bicycles, the owner used to give me textile-related work. He gave me Khaki shirts and pant-cutting jobs. I learnt how to cut 200 shirts at a time by laying layers of fabric on a huge table and cut the 200 shirts or pants with a hand knife. I did not have any problems in learning the job. I mastered the cutting skill in two weeks' time.

The owner of business was Gulabbhai Naik, a well-settled businessman and devotee of Aurobindo, who was a human god married to a French woman—who was called a Goddess—at Aurobindo Ashram of Pondicherry, South India.

I had to leave the job because I received an Army training call from the Rhodesian Government, under the British rule.

The Lord's blessing on me:

Army Training in September of 1957

When I was in Luanshya, (Zambia) I got a call for compulsory army training.

I went to the British Army for training. This was a compulsory military training for all young residents of Northern Rhodesia. On September 7th, 1957, the military airplane flew us to Bulawayo, Southern Rhodesia (now Zimbabwe). The army flight was my first flying experience. It was like sitting on a bench with canvas seats in a straight row. The flight was full of young boys of about my age. We were flown to the Bulawayo Army airstrip. As the plane landed and the door opened, there was a big shout, "Come on! Double-up." I did not know the meaning of 'double up'. I saw that the boys started running in the direction of a military truck. I followed them. The truck took us to the Llewellyn barracks at a place called Heaney, 18 miles from Bulawayo.

There, we were not given any chance to relax. I heard a man shouting at us all the time, with filthy words. We were taken to a huge warehouse where lots of other recruits were lined up. We stood in line and there, I saw a man giving trainees injections in the arms. He was injecting like he was playing darts. I was scared but I had no choice but to take the injection.

Immediately, we were asked to go to another warehouse to get our clothing and boots. It was hot weather and with all the running and having taken a shot in one hand, I had pain in my left hand. There, we were given a duffle bag to put our clothing in. The boots had tie-up leather laces. I put one on my shoulder and another one in the duffle bag.

I reached our barrack. I chose my bed in the middle of the barrack, in front of a Gujarati boy. Other recruits were of mixed race. In the South African and Rhodesian language, they were called coloreds. All of them were local and they drank beer every day. I was not happy with the situation but the Gujarati boy, who grew up in Bulawayo, said not to worry about them.

The next day, two colored boys came to me asking for money and started quarrelling with me. At that time, a tall *Kathiawadi* (South-Gujarati) boy saw me struggling with them. He was in the senior squad. He came to me and asked me what happened. I told him that they were demanding money from me. He held them by their necks and threw them away. He swore at them in Gujarati. He was not good in English but he was strong and tall. He warned them and told them not to touch me. From then, the *Kathiawadi* became my friend.

The training was tough and the rules of the British Army were very strict with respect to the law of color—discriminating against the non-white. We were given full training but all Indian and Colored (mix races of black and white) were given Service and transport jobs in the SNT Platoon. We had to learn to drive army trucks of up to 30 tons, the armored vehicles and military buses. I drove armor tanks and trucks and specialized in vehicles with the clutch paddle between the accelerator and the brake paddles. It was called a 4 X 4 (four by four) vehicle. A vehicle with a unique gear-changing device was given to me because I'd mastered it.

I learned to fire the rifle, pistol, stand gun, bren gun with a tripod and the LMG (light machine gun).

The training was done with rifles and bayonets, punching bags, crawling into narrow holes, jumping on walls, hanging onto ropes and jumping the walls plus physical training like walking in a line in full battle uniform with rifles. We fired at nearby and faraway targets during firing-range training. At our final test at firing, I was almost the winner but I missed a small moving target and another boy made it.

On top of the training, I was given extra responsibilities.

I was in charge of mail collection and distribution. I had good chances of finding out who was getting snack parcels from home. There were some married guys who got parcels and letters. I used to ask them if they wanted the letter or the snacks. Obviously, it was just a friendly game! I gave them the letter first and then the parcel. The friends used to share their goodies with me. I had another duty—of keeping records of laundry dispatch and receipt. The Sargeant liked my handwriting. So, he gave me this extra duty, too. I did all that plus my training. I used to keep myself very busy.

During Diwali (a Hindu festival) time, all my Indian friends were given two days' leave. They did not grant me leave because I had a Christian name. I wanted to go to the city with my friends for the long weekend plus take two extra days' leave. I also wanted to see Bulawayo city.

One of my friends said that I should go to the sickbay and say that I have severe toothache. They may give me leave. I tried that and went to the clinic. I had to sit in attention because the doctor was a Sergeant Major. I told him my problems. He did not say anything and did not even check my teeth. He went inside his office and returned shortly. He came out with a plier-like instrument and asked me which one hurt. I showed him the tooth. He used an injection and with a plier and pulled my teeth out. I had no choice but to accept whatever he did.

Now, I had more pains but he did not allow me to take leave. He asked me to go to back to doing my normal duties. I walked about a mile because it was target-shooting day. I walked in the heat; I was tired. I had more pain than before with the extraction of two teeth. I was bleeding from my mouth.

At the shooting range, I was given a stand gun to practice with. Stand guns were very light. I thought I could fire it with one hand but the instructor showed me how to hold the stand gun because it was more powerful than the ordinary rifles. I was given 30 round magazines to fire. I thought that it would be a piece of cake but when I pulled the trigger, the gun was so powerful that I nearly shot my own toe. I was holding the gun like a toy but it was real. The instructor helped hold the gun and asked me to pull the trigger. The stand gun was very hard to handle if you had no practice. I learnt firing the Stand-gun. It is a gun that fired 30 rounds in a few minutes. On one side, the bullets fired and on the other side—the right side—hot bullet blanks come out. I was still bleeding from my mouth.

One of the colored men gave me a cigarette and asked me to smoke it to stop the bleeding and pain. I was willing to do anything to stop the bleeding. I started puffing the smoke. I did not know the cigarettes were injurious to health. It was hot on that day; I had facial pain and I was still bleeding. I was feeling dizzy because of the cigarette's tobacco. I think the Lord punished me for pretending to be sick for taking leave. Not only did I not get leave, I also had immense pain. I remembered, "Thou shalt not lie."

The training was almost over but just then, we had our outside duties assigned to us. We had to be in full battlefield uniform, with a 9-pound rifle, and walk for miles. We walked about 20 miles in one day, under the hot sun. It was fun initially, but not afterwards, as we were walking through the jungle thinking of all the animals that could appear and attack us from behind or the front made me scared. The rifle, with a heavy backpack, woolen socks and heavy army boots, was getting heavier. The sun had not set yet but my hopes of reaching my destination were setting.

When we returned back to our barracks, I threw everything on my bed and went straight for the cold-water shower. After cooling down, I wore very light clothing and walked half a mile for my dinner. There, I drank my usual

"Hubbly-Bubbly" pineapple drink. I sat with my friends for dinner. No one spoke much because we were all tired from walking. After dinner, we walked slowly to the barracks.

The following week, we had to drive toward Gwelo city (now Gweru), on the gravel road. There was a main road, which was tarred, but our army truck training was to drive on jungle roads. We were driving with a co-driver. This time, the truck was empty. I was allocated one truck though I had no army-driving license. My Sergeant was sitting by me as my co-driver. I told him that I had no license. He said I was driving fine.

We were driving in convoy. I was the leading truck. I had to drive all the way to Gwelo, which was about 95 miles. We reached Gwelo and sat by the roadside near Gwelo town. We were not given any lunch. I had my water bottle in my truck.

After about an hour in Gwelo, we returned back on the same road. It was training to drive in convoy in the jungle.

It was about 4 PM when I was driving on the rough road; I drove over some sharp stone. Both the offside tires were blown. They were actually cut badly because of the heat. The steering wheel became very hard to control but the co-driver, the Sergeant, helped me in controlling it. The whole convoy stopped behind my truck.

I had only one spare wheel. My Sergeant jumped into another truck. I was told to wait with the truck and that he would send a spare wheel with someone. I was alone in the truck, in the jungle, under the hot, hot sun. I was tired, scared and hungry. I was running out of water in my bottle. This was an unexpected problem. I gathered courage, looked around and walked to a tree for shade. I was looking out for the danger of wild animals. There was no way I could sit in the stationery truck under the hot sun. There was no air-conditioner in the army truck. Those days, air-conditions hadn't been invented for vehicles.

At about 6 PM, help came. The mechanic fitted the tire. We returned to our barracks in 20 minutes. It was already time for my dinner, so I rushed to the canteen and had my dinner and Pineapple drink.

On that day, I was very tired, so I slept early. I wrote about the incident to my dad and in turn, as usual, he wrote lots of advices. The main advice is still in my memory: *'Fast in bend brings the end.'* The next day was Sunday. I was sleeping with the blanket over my face, listening to Indian music.

At that time, someone pulled my blanket and asked me what I was doing? "It's Sunday—let's go to Bulawayo," he said. It was the brother-in-law of my friend, Kanji Parmer. With a little introduction, we became friendly. He had come from Bulawayo just to pick me up for Sunday lunch with his family.

The brother-in-law was Mr. Parshottam Giga, and his wife, Dhaniben, who was originally from Ndola. She told me that my dad knew his family and that he often visited them in Ndola. I then remembered visiting the family. I did not know her because she was already married and living in Bulawayo.

They'd cooked a nice meal. I felt like having food that was just like my mum's cooking.

They insisted that I come every weekend to visit them. Parshottam said that he would come and pick me up. I was given the weekend off because I'd almost finished my training. They were a big family of three married brothers living under one roof. Although they had separate areas, they lived in one house. They ate their meals in the same dining room. I became a part of their family. Every weekend, they used to cook food exactly like how my mom did, in Bombay. No wonder, my mum was also from Kathiawar, like the Giga family.

Mr. Parshottam Giga became my best friend and his wife, Dhaniben, became like my sister; she was from my town, Ndola.

I really enjoyed my last days in the army training camp. We were seniors. We had a passing-out parade for our last salute to the senior-most officer of the training 2-IC (Second-in-command).

At the army, I was paid on the last day my accumulated wages. It was 15 pounds a month—which I did not take. At the end of the training, I collected the wages. All my money was given to my dad. In return, he bought me a white shirt SK22, of Egyptian cotton, and a nylon suit. He bought it at CAMCO, the company in which he worked. I remember it even now because that was the only gift I ever got from my dad.

Thereafter, I was a businessman. I used to sell varieties of clothing in my shop; I could give him clothing as a gift.

After the Army Training

I joined my dad at Dhirubhai's home. At that time, the Lord made me an army and civilian driver, and made me physically strong. My English accent had changed, too. I started shaving my beard and became a young man. I do not remember how my teen years passed. I feel that I skipped my childhood and directly landed into old age. I did not enjoy my teenage years; neither did I enjoy in my youth because I started working in my teens and worked till the age of retirement, with lots of responsibilities and hardships.

I was now a reservist in the army. We had to attend training in our city. I was in Ndola.

There was compulsory army training every weekend. We had to be ready with our army clothing at all times because they could call us for any emergencies or war.

At one time, I was assigned to go to Kitwe, a copper-mining town. Ndola to Kitwe was about 40 miles. I had to go at 9 PM to the army office and get orders from the officer. I took my truck and drove to Kitwe all by myself. At Kitwe, I reached O.B. Bennet hall.

In Kitwe, I was given the duty of taking care of the road leading to the Congo border. I went there at about midnight and waited to see the refugees coming with left-hand-driven, long cars with Belgian-Congo number plates. I had to stand like a traffic officer to stop the cars and guide them to O.B. Bennet hall. From the border to the hall, it was about 30 miles. I stood at the fork of the road to stop the cars and guide the European families of Belgian origin to the hall.

I had a very bad experience that day. The Belgian government gave independence to the African-majority government. The Africans, who were freedom fighters, were hiding in the jungle with lots of dangerous weapons. They came out as they got the right to self-government and started killing the Europeans residents. The families fled from the country and escaped to Zambia.

At that time, Zambia was called Northern Rhodesia, under President Ian Smith, who declared a unilateral government defending the British rule. The government was still called British but the minority—the white supremists who were discriminative against the local Africans or non-whites—were ruling the Federal government. That was called the Federation of Rhodesia and Nyasaland (Nyasaland is now Malawi).

All the refugees that came by me, I saw, were crying and some of them were injured. They all came empty-handed. My job was to help them and take the refugees from the Belgian-Congo border to O.B. Bennet hall.

I met a car, which had injured parents and a girl in severe pain. I took them to the hospital in Kitwe. They were French-speaking people, but they could speak some English. The parents were victims of the gangs with *pangas* (bladed, big, tool-like African machete). They took the girl and eight of those wild blacks raped her. She was in a serious condition. I had to leave them at the hospital with instructions that they must report to the Rhodesian Army officer at O.B. Bennet Hall.

I don't know what happened to that girl. But I was very nervous and scared too. It was in the jungle of Congo, though I was on the Rhodesian side of the border. I was not worried about the wild animals because I had my Rifle with the Bayonet on it but it was difficult to fight Congo's guerilla army. The DRC (Democratic Republic of Congo) took over the government.

When Belgium's government realized that Congo was ungovernable, they initiated the round-table talks that led to its independence in 1960. After independence, the black guerilla army emerged from the jungle and started looting the whites' residences and killing them.

The refugees came without anything but escaped with their big, long, left-hand-driven cars. In Zambia, we were driving right-hand cars so I was amazed to see the line of unique-looking cars coming through the Congo and Zambia border.

Under the guerilla army of free Congo, and a new black government, there was no safety for the Belgian people. Congo was under Belgian rule. But when they gave independence, they did not know the guerilla army would begin massacring the whites. The sad part of it was that young girls and boys were in big danger—I have seen bad scenes and devastated families.

I directed them to O.B. Bennet hall in Kitwe for their shelter, food and first aid. Some of the young girls and boys were taken to the hospital directly and some of them died. I saw this at a very young age. Army training is not for killing rivals but it is for taking care of the citizens and defending the country. I worked for one week at Kitwe and returned home.

The following month, I was called to go to Chingola, a Zambian city near the Congo border. Usually, the army's instructions were not clear. They just ordered us to go and wait for another order. It was in the winter of 1961 when I was told to drive to Solwezi town, near the Congo border. I had to drive through the thick jungles of Congo.

At that time, we did not know where we are going. I was not even a licensed driver. I did not have an army license. I told the sergeant who assigned me to drive to the Solwezi village that I was not licensed. I was trying to avoid driving but somehow he liked me and he was very polite with me. He said that I was a driver and should just drive. He sat with me.

We drove in a four-trucks convoy with 42 soldiers at the back of the truck and some food items, too. I sat with my rifle, fully loaded and bayoneted. If the enemy attacked the convoy, they killed the driver first. I was driving with the fear of the Congo guerilla attacking us. That night, we reached Solwezi—the last town of Zambia near Congo. We were given no food; just some vegetable cans, tins of fish and cheese. I was not hungry because I was scared of the jungle and the Congo guerilla army.

We did not change our clothing; we slept with our boots on and our caps on our head with our weapon on our side. In the morning, the sentry on duty—a fellow soldier who had kept the fire going—had a pot with hot water to prepare coffee for us. I did not have anything to eat or water to drink for the three days that I spent in fear on the journey. I was eating cheese and tinned sardines. The next morning, we were all chatting and cracking jokes with each other when I began having severe abdominal pain. I told one of the Indian friends that I had not passed water for three days. One of the soldiers was drinking beer; he came to me with a can of beer and told me to sip it. I'd never had any kind of liquor in my life. I refused to take it. He said he was giving me the beer as a medicine for my problems. I took the beer and drank it all in one gulp. In five minutes, I passed water and felt much better. I drank another can to get over my physical problems and clear my kidneys. I was feeling much better. I was seriously worried sick because I had not passed water, but God sent His help to me there too, in the jungles of Congo.

The next morning, there was an order for us to go further into the jungle. We were not told where we were heading. I was assigned as a driver by the same sergeant who accompanied me from Chingola. I wanted to avoid driving because I did not have a military license. I asked the sergeant to take some other driver with him but he insisted that I drive. Reluctantly, I joined the convoy of four trucks. I was the last truck. I had my rifle with bayonet mounted on it, ready to fire, but I had only five bullets in my magazine. We started at about 8 AM. At about 10 AM, we reached a Tsetse flies barrier, where we had to drive our truck through chemical water and the truck was sprayed so that Tsetse flies couldn't come near. From there, we drove in a sharp curve, going downhill. At the edge of the hill, there was a sharp turn on the left. Upon turning left, there was a bridge with two planks on a swinging rope. I was shocked and was scared going on that clumsy bridge. I was in third gear, driving the 30-ton truck with 42 soldiers—all were screaming looking at that dangerous bridge. I was so scared that I might fall off the bridge. The bridge was crossed and the steep hill came. That was another danger. For the heavy truck to go uphill on such a steep hill, I had to change my gear to the first and climb slowly, with fear that it may not have the power to climb the hill while fully loaded. I was praying in my heart to my Lord to help me. But God was with me. I made it on the mountain safely. All the soldiers cheered and called out to me, saying, "Bravo, Bravo."

I was driving along when suddenly I felt that my steering was not responding well. It had gone loose. I told the Sargeant that there were some problems with the steering wheel. The Sargeant said that I had made it across the most dangerous road with the same steering, so I had nothing to worry about. In half an hour, the truck that was going on the straight road pulled itself on one side. The nut holding the steering rod got loose and I could not control the truck. But I applied a sharp break and stopped the truck. God helped me stop in a strange spot. One side was a sharp slope and the other side was a big hole—my truck stood right in between the two. The soldiers jumped out of the truck and came running to me and asked me how I was feeling. I drank a full bottle of water and wiped my sweaty face. It was hot in the jungles of Congo, which is on the line of the Equator.

My sergeant said that I was right about the steering wheel. All the four trucks had stopped and a mechanic came to check them. He did minor repairs and he drove the truck. It was severely cold at night and sunny and hot in the daytime. We reached the Kolwezi border of Congo. Kolwezi is a famous place because the Zambezi River starts from there.

We reached the border at about 6 PM and slept there with our uniforms, boots and jungle hat on at the back of the truck. This was the fourth day that we had not removed the woolen army socks and boots. The following morning, when I woke up, I saw that we were camping at the edge of a beautiful river. There was a small waterfall with clean mineral water and it was a sunny day but the water was nice and cool. I went to the river and sat on a rock. I untied my bootlaces and took my stinking socks off. I was shocked to see that my skin was rotting and peeling out. I put my leg in the cool water, but it was like a shock on my leg. I pulled my leg out and dipped it in again several times, till I was comfortable. It was nice to be at the river. The camping area was beautiful. The other soldiers had their tents organized in line. Our trucks were camouflaged. The greenery around was amazing. It was a nice camping spot.

My Court Martial

After breakfast, there was a call for me. The officer in charge, 2 IC, set a court for my court-martial. I was asked to come into a tent for attending the military court. I had to get in a special uniform and come drilling to the officer. There were four officers sitting but I had to stand in attention. One of them asked me what had happened at the accident. I was strong; I did not have any fear so I told them that the steering was faulty which was reported to the Sergeant. The Sergeant gave his testimony and the mechanic pledged, too, that the steering was loose. I was released but the officer asked me to go back to the Solwezi camp to get more supplies. I told them that I need a co-driver for my long journey. I was given a helper who was a Gujarati friend and he was a good driver, too. He had a military license and had good driving experience. I asked him to drive but he was not assigned for the truck. I took the truck and, after driving for about 50 miles, I told him to take over. This was easy because there was no officer with us. We drove happily through the jungle, chatting and singing Hindi songs. We stopped by a jungle shop to buy soda and biscuits. The Tsetse flies area bridge was scary but I was not worried because the truck was empty. Finally, we reached Solwezi camp in the evening, at about 6 PM. There, Indian friends prepared some good Indian tinned-fish curry and rice. We celebrated the night because the commanding officers were not there. The sergeants were very friendly. There was no color discrimination; they were drinking beer from cans and the whole environment was like an evening party full of musical entertainment, but the next day, I had to return to Kolwezi with some supplies. The truck was not heavy because the supplies were very little.

I was a little fearful because I was supposed to go back to Kolwezi through the same route. I took another driver with me and I went back—singing and eating well—to the Kolwezi camp. I took some arms and ammunition, some beer and soda supplies and some canned food. I sat by the river in the morning but there, I was awoken by a call for an emergency. We had to go to the border, where we had some cross-firing going on. We had to camouflage our truck and ourselves. To fight with guerilla fighters was frightening but we were trained for it. I had no problems because I was under the protection of my Lord. The Lord was everywhere, protecting me in all circumstances.

After four years in the army—the British Army—the order was stopped and Northern Rhodesia became Zambia under President Kenneth Kaunda. The British rule was overthrown and the new government took over and renamed it Zambia.

14 February 1958
(Start of My Own Business)

When I came back home from the border, the Lord gave me another task. I started a small shop of my own. The shop was going very well. I had some prior experience selling in the retail shop and I bought some goods from the wholesalers and from distributors. I started the business and as it was going well, there was a proposal from the friend, where my dad was living with as a paying guest. The business was the same as mine but his shop was in the middle of the city, whereas my shop was at one end of the city. We merged the businesses and started a partnership. My dad wanted me to be with someone elderly and more mature in business.

With our partnership, the business started picking up with the blessings of our Lord.

It so happened, that a priest of an African church having services in the local Bemba language was doing his high school studies. He came to our English-service church and gave a message to the congregation. He met us at the church. He became very friendly with us and asked us to come and visit his house, which was in the same area as the African Church.

My dad and I went there while he was doing his studies. He was battling with his Algebra and Geometry lessons. We saw that he needed help; my dad helped him with his math lessons. After that, he started coming to our house for his tuitions. My dad helped him with his studies but when my dad was not at home, I helped him with his math. He graduated and went on to study theology in South India. He visited our home in Bombay. We became close friends. When he returned back to Ndola, he told my dad that he needed some school uniforms made.

My dad came with an order to supply the school uniforms for the Christian-run school. Seeing the uniforms made by us, the manager of school, a member of the African Church, asked the priest about the makers of the uniforms. He gave him our names. Then, we had a meeting with the manager of the schools at the African church on the following Saturday. The manager of the school gave us orders to make uniforms for all the schools in Ndola.

This was the biggest opportunity for our business. I had the fabric laid out on a huge table and my cutting skills from my Luanshya job came in handy. So, it was easy for us to make the uniforms. We decided to close the shop, which was out of the city, and concentrate on our city shop plus the uniform-making tailoring unit in one side of the shop.

When schools opened, a flood of customers came rushing for the uniforms. We did not have machines to make large quantities. We had only four machines and four machinists. We were a small tailoring business, but when the crowd of people came to the shop for buying uniforms, we were shocked. We had to close the doors to prevent the rush. We told the crowd that the uniforms would be supplied directly to the schools. The people went back. There were two thousand people shouting and asking for uniforms. The street was flooded with uniform buyers.

We started looking for machinists to operate the machines. We did not have machines but the machinists that came looking for work could come with their own machines and we gave them jobs. In one week's time, we had 20 machines and machinists. They were happy to get the jobs and got money for every garment they made. We imported a good amount of fabric and spoke to the manager of schools, asking him to hold on for a while for the uniforms. We told him that we would supply the uniforms in three months' time. We worked day and night, prepared the uniforms and supplied in thousands.

Our business flourished from the house of our Lord—the blessed African church. When schools opened, we had police guarding the streets and keeping buyers in discipline. We were only two of us doing all the selling. At that time, Augustine came from India to join my business.

Lilayi Trading Company, trading as Samuel Store

My dad saw an advertisement, which said that there were two plots on sale near the Police Training School. The plots are offered only to those connected with the Police department. My dad applied for a plot, quoting his previous experience with the Police department. We were offered the plot with very little payment for it.

The other plot was offered to Mr. Bhukhan of Bhukhan Tailors, Lusaka. They were Army/Police uniform makers.

The Lord was in our favor all the time. We were given the plot near a police training school, about 10 miles from the city of Lusaka, the Capital city of Zambia. It was in a rural area and non-citizens could not get plots in rural areas.

Being the first Indian Christian, dad had good standing in our church in Ndola. My partner and my dad decided to build a shop on that plot. We gave the work to a builder in Lusaka and he built the shop in six months' time.

I visited the plot a couple of times when the shop was being built and went to meet the police officers at the training school. The place was called Lilayi Police Training School. So, I named the shop as Lilayi trading company, trading as 'Samuel Store.'

When the shop was ready, the partner and I were supposed to go and start the business but the partner played his card. He told me to go and take over the shop and that he would take care of the shop in Ndola.

The Ndola shop was going very well so, very cleverly, he asked for dissolving the partnership. Profits from the Ndola business went to him and the Lusaka business came to me but the building was listed as my share. He spoke to me rudely just to get me out of the business partnership. My dad was helpless because we lived with him. This was another good plan of my Lord.

It was getting harder and harder to deal with the partner and his household. I took up the challenge to go to Lusaka. Very little was shown as my share in the books of accounts, so he gave me the old station Wagon and five pounds to fill gas. I had some empty bottles of soda, which I loaded into my van because I needed the weight to drive on certain gravel roads with two tracks.

I reached Lusaka and went to a friend, Mr. Ratilal Shah's home. He had already offered me accommodation—to come and stay with him when I visited Lusaka. He and his wife were very good to me. She cooked very good food and treated me like I was her brother. At the end of the month, I offered to pay him but he did not take money from me. He was a primary school teacher and used to repair radios in his spare time—a real gentleman. I blessed the couple from the bottom of my heart. I was given one room with a comfortable bed. My problem was solved automatically. Now, I was well-settled with good accommodation and good food. I had the vehicle but I had very little money. I sold the empty soda bottles and got two pounds for it. The next day, I went to the shop and saw that the shop was ready with wooden shelves and counters. I was happy to start. I went to Lusaka city and visited the distributors and wholesale businesses to give me some goods on credit. I had no security to offer but I had my Lord as security.

Life in Lusaka

In the path of life, we meet many individuals. I travelled extensively; so, I have met many individuals. The memories of some individuals are printed in my mind, which is still intact in me. I remember all the occasions and people like it all happened yesterday. That is why I am writing all my memories here as my history and my family's history as I remember it.

I worked very hard, facing tough challenges, setbacks and painful incidents and suffered physically—which I still do; I have sleepless nights.

As I wrote these memories, I dropped tears remembering my problems—because I was alone with no one to help. I was hungry; I was lonely but bore difficulties remembering my family back in India. I was only a teenager when I was the only Indian Christian in Lusaka and youngest individual in the businessman community. Today, I think that I was not alone; my Lord was with me and through His grace, I sailed safely through the ocean of agony.

I had my own retail business at the Lilayi Police Training area, Lusaka. I used to start working early in the morning. I had no one to rebuke me but I was strict with myself. I always remembered my dad's words: "Early to bed and early to rise is the way to be healthy, wealthy and wise." I was out in the city, at suppliers' places, at 8 AM. The wholesale businessmen and other suppliers helped me start my business when I had only seven pounds in my pocket. They were Mr. Bhagat, Mr. Adambhai Badat, who was the commissioner of Oath and a Lusaka council member and Mr. Kashibhai Patel, who was the Mayor of Broken Hill (now Kabwe). He had his own wholesale business. He was a very strict individual but he was like a father to me in terms of business. He loved me; he rebuked me for any wrongdoing.

One day, I went wearing full-length pants without turning them up. In those days, the style was to have a turn-up hemming at the bottom of the pant. He rebuked me and said I had a new fever! I was embarrassed so I went home, changed my pants and returned to him. He laughed and said I looked good.

I am proudly mentioning these names because these people counted me as their own son and supplied goods without any security. They gave me goods to fill my shop and they did not demand money. How could this be and how did it happen to me? They did not know me and did not ask me who I was. God worked behind me and He was with me all the time.

On Sunday, I used to attend church in the morning and after that, at about noon, I drove to my shop to earn money because I had to meet my payments to my creditors.

On Sundays, I used to pass by Hindu Hall in Lusaka where there were Indian movie shows. I used to pass by the place not looking at it, but looking past it. I did not turn to look at the crowd waiting for movie, lest I feel like going to the movie and lose business and spend money equivalent to a day's meal for my family.

The suppliers' saw my courage and my willpower; they offered me to take whatever I wanted from the stock. About three wholesalers told me the same. I was wondering why people were more inclined to help me and spoke very nicely to me. They even said pay when you can. Usually, wholesalers needed their payments in 30 to 90 days but I was given goods with open terms—this was the Lord's blessing. I had no money so I had to work hard to get some money from sales.

The business started and I did well from the first day. I used to go shopping in the morning for some daily-perishable items and other textile goods. The other commodities, in bigger quantities, I used to buy during the weekends. I used to reach my shop at about 10 AM. Being in a rural area, and especially near the police training school, this was a good timing. I worked the whole day without any lunch break—sometimes till 11 PM at the end of the month. I used to close the shop at 10 PM usually, taking all the cash with me in a big bag and driving to the city.

On the way, I used to stop at a drive-in café and park my car at one corner. As soon as I parked my car at that particular spot, a server ran to my car and placed a table beside my car's window. He brought my daily menu—one cheese and tomato sandwich with a cup of hot coffee. That was my only meal for the whole day. At lunchtime, I used to eat a one-penny bun and drink a bottle of Coca Cola. This was my daily routine.

One day, I was tired of eating buns. I decided to fry an egg. I had a primus stove and a frying pan in my shop. I brought an oil bottle and eggs to fry for lunch. I started the primus stove and placed the pan on it. I filled half the pan with oil. When the oil was hot, I dropped the egg in it. But, to my surprise, the egg started flying everywhere. I had to turn off the stove. I thought about how mum cooked eggs. I realized that there was too much oil in the pan. So, I took the oil out and dropped the egg in the oily pan. The egg was cooked but slightly burnt. So, I reduced the flame, put a little more oil again and dropped another egg in it. That egg was cooked well. That day, I was able to afford to eat another menu but that was not possible every day.

I did well at my shop and paid all my dues in time. I filled more stock and my business flourished. After three months, my dad asked me to send 300 pounds to help my partner as he was in trouble. I immediately sent a check for 300 pounds to him. I don't think he needed the money; he just wanted to check on the status of my accounts.

God was helpful to me all the time. My brother had a rough time with the family. When I visited Ndola, I could see that my brother was in jeopardy. I asked dad if I could take my brother with me. My brother was very happy to come with me. I was surviving on Coke and one-penny buns but I did not want my brother to suffer the same. I did not know how to get good food for him.

At that time, God looked at my problems. One elderly person Mr. Bhaget, a supplier, asked me what I did for my meals. I told him that I did not know cooking so I had been surviving on sandwiches. He invited me home to have a meal with him. I told him my timing was not suitable and that it was not possible. He said that he had a cook who could cook delicious food.

God works in mysterious ways. How did the supplier, Mr. Bhagat, know about my food problems? How did he get the idea of asking me about my food problems? I needed a cook to take care of my brother.

I employed the cook named Ario. He was an excellent cook. He cooked such good food that my brother always used to give him a list of all the food he wanted. The food problem was solved by itself, by the grace of God.

Augustine learnt driving in Ndola with me, and now he had business training as well. He used to work with me and seem very happy. He became a good driver and met some friends at Lusaka club.

In December 1965, my dad asked me to go to India and get married. I was not prepared but my two sisters and my older brother were married already and I was next in line. Augustine was already trained to take care of the business. He had friends also to give him company.

It was not necessary to get married leaving the business, but Augustine was now ready to take up the responsibilities. In the Eastern culture, we usually have arranged marriages. It is just like how Jacob had to marry the older daughter of Laban because the customary law was that Rachel could not marry him when Leah, her elder sister, was not married. We go by the same rule in Eastern countries, although it is not a law. We follow such things blindly as far as possible. I booked a ticket to go to India in December of 1965.

I was worried about my naive brother because the shop was in remote area where facilities were not adequate. The Lilayi post office was inside Police camp. The phone was on a party line—there were 10 phones on one line—but each phone had its own ringtone. My ringtone was two long rings and one short one. If I picked up the calls of others, I could hear all their conversations. I have gone through all kinds of experiences while living the rural life. I had to encounter some bad villagers, too.

All the police recruits in Zambia were trained at the Lilayi training school. I was well-known to them all. I spoke to the Police camp officer-in-charge, to take care of my brother. He assured me of his safety. Wherever I went, I used to find policemen identifying me. Especially at the immigration border, I had special treatment. I once went to a remote area of Zambia; there also I was known. My dad was known in Bombay city; I was well-known in the whole of Zambia and honored by the police officers, including the President's special security police.

My Prayer answered

This is my testimony for people to know that God was, is and will always be ever-living. He answers our prayers. I have personally experienced it. I am writing this as proof that the Lord moved for an ordinary person like me just because I prayed for His help. He answered my prayer in such a way that by reading my testimony, many would turn to the true God. The Lord moves in our lives in amazing ways.

My Testimony

One day, when I was alone at the shop, something moved me. I shut the front door at lunchtime and went into the back room, where I had my little office and the warehouse. I lay a straw mat on the ground, took a Bible and started reading. I was given the chapter 24 of the book of Genesis. Amazingly, this was not arranged but I read the chapter and prayed.

My Prayer

"That like Abraham trusted his servant for a bride for his son Isaac, I trust you Lord that you will go before me to find a bride of your choice for me because I have not much time for selection of a girl."

My prayer just came up on my lips and I spoke to the Lord. At this time, I was thinking of the old hymn 'take it to the Lord in prayers.' Thoughts came in my mind about how I worked very hard for this business and it was going well; how I was leaving it to my naïve brother to be taken care of. But in my prayer, I asked the Lord to take care of the shop and of my brother. I do not remember the whole prayer and details of whatever I said to the Lord; I just want to bear witness to the fact that the Lord was faithful and helpful to me wherever I went.

Visit to India 1965 (for marriage)

On the 5th of December 1965, I started my journey from Lusaka, on a flight, to Dar-Es'-Salaam. I sat at the allocated window seat; next to me, a young Indian man came and sat.

We spoke the same language. I found out that he was the manager of Zambia Aluminum Company. He was the son of the Chandaria family—one of the biggest businessmen and well-known tycoons of Tanzania. He became good friends with me and offered that I come and stay at his home in Dar-Es'-Salaam. But I had other arrangements; two businessmen were waiting for me at the airport.

When we disembarked from the flight, I was the first in line at the Immigration counter. The officer looked at me and threw my passport on the ground like it was some garbage. I was furious and wanted to see what he had done to my passport. But at that time, Chandaria—who was standing behind me—asked me to me keep calm and said that he would handle it.

He cleared his immigration procedures and went straight to the officer-in-charge. He gave him a gift to grant me one-day visa because I was a transit passenger.

I was supposed to stay in Dar-Es'-Salaam for four days because the next flight was scheduled for Nairobi four days after.

In those days, there were no frequent flights. I had to stop in Dar-Es'-Salaam and thence go to Nairobi; and from Nairobi to Ethiopia, and after a halt at Eden, finally to Bombay. I was first in line at the immigration but was cleared last. God sent His help to me and took me safely to Dar-Es'-Salaam.

Two friends were waiting for me at the arrivals, but I was delayed at the immigration.

They were the most hospitable people; the family members were very entertaining. I felt like I was at home. I was a guest of Chunilal Dusara's family, who had an electronic goods business and their eldest brother, Tribhuvan Dusara, was a member of the ruling political party.

The next day, they took me to the Immigration office and, with their influence, got me a visa for four days. I then found out what the reason was for my passport getting thrown at the airport.

It so happened that on that day, the people of Tanzania, because of some diplomatic fallout, had pelted stones at the British government offices and Embassy. I landed with my British passport the same evening. After getting four days' extension, I went to the British Embassy to get an Emergency passport but they could not issue a passport because the office was closed for business. The officer asked me to approach the Nairobi office.

Anyway, I was well protected by my Lord. I had a nice air-conditioned room where I slept very comfortably. In the morning, I was awakened by the loud noise of the Muslim prayer. Initially, I was scared of the loud noise; the man was shouting through the loudspeaker in such a way that I thought he was in my room. I knew that it was the Muslim Namaz (Prayer) time. I slept well and got up with the prayers although it was Muslim Azan prayers. I got ready. The family gave me a good breakfast and excellent hospitality. They took me around and showed me the whole of the city. I saw the University of Tanzania, too.

In Dar-Es'-Salaam, the Dusaras knew of a Christian lady from a Gujarati-speaking family.

They took me to her place because she was a teacher in the school where he was a student. I was dropped at the teacher's house. She had a daughter—a candidate for marriage. The family was good. The time I was at their house was 4 pm. The daughter was sleeping. The lady went and woke her up to meet me. Needless to say, she wanted to propose for marriage. I was not ready for anything like that and I spoke nicely with them. The mother was born in the same city where I was born—Surat. We had a good conversation about Christian life in Tanzania. Then, I asked them about a family I knew, John Paltanwalla. The lady said that she knew them very well. So, she asked the daughter to take me to their place. The girl was nice and educated and she was a very good person. She told me about the Church in Dar-Es'-Salaam. They were members of the Anglican Church. We reached the house of John Paltanwalla but he was not there. His son, about my age, met me and talked to me about our family connections. I had a good chat with them and they entertained me well at their house. The girl was so good that she waited for me and took me to Chunilal Dusara's house, where I was staying.

Thereafter, I never met the family.

From Dar-Es'-Salaam, I boarded the flight to Nairobi on the fourth day. The flight was small; it halted for about half an hour at Arusha airport. Arusha airport was so small that there was only 1 airstrip there and there was no building. They had a hut made of gum-poles as the airport's building. I sat on a gum pole for about 20 minutes and boarded the aircraft. As the flight took-off, I saw the Kilimanjaro Mountain for the first time with the white sheet spread on it. I reached Nairobi.

At the airport, I had a suspicion that my passport may be thrown like it was in Tanzania. I was in line at the immigration desk. I saw the immigration officer—a Sikh-Indian officer—and hoped that I got a chance to go to him because he may help me with my passport. The Lord answered my prayer. The same Indian immigration officer called me to come up to him. I tendered my passport with full confidence that that officer would not throw my passport away. After checking my passport, he gave me four days' entry but he quietly told me to go immediately to the British Embassy and get an emergency passport. I took my baggage and boarded the Kenya Airlines bus and reached their city terminal.

I was supposed to go to the New Stanley hotel, which was a little far from the terminal. So, when I saw the Ambassador Hotel right across the city terminal, it was convenient for me to cross the road and reach the hotel. I went in and found a nice room in the hotel. I relaxed for half a day and went out into the city to get some Indian food.

I was supposed to be meeting a family for a marriage proposal. My dad had arranged for me to meet a girl of a certain family. I expected them to come and meet me at the airport but instead of coming to the airport, they came to meet me at the New Stanly hotel, which was arranged by my dad. They did not find me there so they thought that I had not come. I had their address. So, on the third day—Saturday afternoon at about 4 PM—I went to their home by taxi. I knocked at the door and a beautiful lady opened the door for me. She immediately recognized me. She was beautifully dressed with a nice facial done and red lipstick on; she had put on some perfume. When I saw her, I thought that she was the girl proposed for me. But then, I found out that she was the mother! The Lord immediately told me that that was not the place for me. My mum and sisters were not as modern when compared to the attitude of that family. I had already decided not to even speak about marriage with the family. The girl was in her room. I was sitting in the lounge. The mother went in and told the girl about me. She dressed up nicely and came with a tray of tea and snacks. The mother told me about the girl and what she was doing. She was looking for a job and she was learning typing. I had no interest in what her activities were. In the meantime, the father came from outside. He had gone out for a walk. He was a very good gentleman. Amazingly, he was from Surat, too. After our family talk, I was ready to go out. The mother said her daughter would drop me at the hotel. I needed the transport so I agreed. She took me in her red Volkswagen (VW) car to the Ambassador Hotel. I asked her to come in for tea but she said that was going for her typing classes. I did not like the looks and behavior of her mother.

In my opinion, engagement is between two families and marriage is the match of two individuals by the blessings and grace of the Lord. There was no match between the two families. The next day was Sunday; I was supposed to go to the nearby church, named St. Andrew Church. The girl's folks were also members of the same church. I went to the church that Sunday morning and met the parents but the girl was not there. After the service was done, I met the parents and they told me that their daughter would be late because she was teaching Sunday school classes. It was very impressive because the girl was nice and she was taking part at the church. But the Lord told me that she was not the girl for me. They asked me about my opinion about the marriage with the girl and I replied calmly that my dad and mum would decide about it and write to them.

I took my flight back on the same day and reached Bombay on Monday morning. At the airport, there were about 100 members of my family waiting for my arrival. I went through the procedures and met my mum and family. I wept loudly, hugging my mum. I met the family after 11 years. I was a 27-year-old young man with a business of my own and had enough money saved from the business. I bought lots of gifts for my family. I reached home and relaxed for the day. My mum asked me about the family in Nairobi and I told her what I saw. My mum was happy because then she had a chance to find a girl for me. I was not worried about whom I was going to marry because I had full confidence in my Lord.

After celebrating Christmas and New Year, my mum started looking for a girl for me.

For a start, there were many girls in our church family but no one came with any proposal. My mum was surprised to see that no family from Bombay came forward with a marriage proposal. The Lord was moving for me.

Uncle Walter's wife, Salome Aunty, came with a proposal and a photo of a girl in Baroda city. I did not know about the girl, but the Lord knew about her. The same week, the girl's grandpa died. So, the girl said that she would only marry the year after. She asked that the boy come again next year. She thought that I would return to Africa and come back for her after one year! The proposal was cancelled. My mum arranged a meeting with a girl in Ahmadabad.

I was supposed to meet the family on Wednesday, the following week. So, Rosemary and I, along with my maternal uncle Walter, decided to go to Bhavnagar to visit my eldest sister Freny as she was married and I'd never met my brother-in-law and had not seen my sister for 11 years. My sister, my uncle and I took a train to go to Bhavnagar. The train journey was via Ahmadabad junction. We reached Ahmadabad at 4.10 PM and from there, we were supposed to take a train to Bhavnagar—which was scheduled for 11 PM.

My uncle asked us to wait at the railway station and went to find my other uncle, my father's younger brother, Wilson Uncle. We waited at the station while Walter uncle went to find Wilson uncle, by rickshaw. Wilson uncle was not married and he was an English-teaching professor at one of the colleges in Ahmadabad. He was about to walk out to meet his other professor friend, who was also unmarried, and have dinner with him.

Both uncles came to the station and I met Wilson uncle after 11 years. When I left India, he was still in college doing his BA degree. Now, he'd become a professor in Gujarat College. From the station, Wilson uncle said that he should go to the friend's house and inform him that he cannot go out today because I'd come. Those days, there were no telephones. Inland letters used to take five days to reach. The four of us went to an area in the big city. The city has a dense population with millions of Christians. The city being big—almost as big as New York City—in area, it was difficult to reach the place. Anyway, after 30 minutes on the rickshaw, we reached a house.

The professor friend lived behind the house and the room was very small. So, he told us to go to the front bungalow where the owner of the house lived and wait for him. He also said that she was an old lady whom he called 'aunty.' This was because he needed to get ready. We went to the front bungalow and Uncle Wilson knocked at the door. At that time, I saw the signboard with the name of the person whose name and address was in my diary—the family I was supposed to meet for the proposal of the marriage. I pulled Walter uncle aside and told him that that was the same place where we were supposed to come on Wednesday. It was too late; the door opened and my uncle greeted the old lady—the granny of the girl I was supposed to meet for marriage. I sat there, looking down and hiding myself. But Uncle Wilson started introducing me as his nephew, who had just arrived from Africa. At that time, the old lady immediately came to me and asked me if I was the same person who was supposed to come to her house on Wednesday. Wilson uncle did not know what was going on but my sister and Walter uncle knew exactly what was happening. This was the Lord's doing that in that huge city, He took me to the house where my marriage was arranged. I spoke to the old lady and she was very pleased with me. The professor friend came and we walked out of the house.

The South Indian-professor friend was from that area and he knew many families there. We walked for about five minutes and at the first corner of the road, the friend told Walter uncle that the family living in that corner house was from Surat. Walter uncle was from Surat, and he knew almost all the Christian families in Surat. So, he walked to the house to find out who they were.

The house door opened and we found that they were Walter uncle's good friends. The lady of the house came out and invited us all in. We went to the house and, as usual, one girl came to serve snacks and tea and the mother started praising her daughter. I told uncle that we should leave because whatever was happening was not good. We were just passing by the road and this lady is already trying to propose the girl to us.

After a few minutes, we left the house and went to my elder brother's brother-in-law's house—where my uncle had kept our baggage. We went to his house. In that neighborhood, there was a girl who was my sister's friend. My sister went there to meet her and knowing that her brother had come from Africa, the girl invited me to her house. My sister came to me and took me to the house. She introduced me to the family. We had a good chat and had some savory food. The girl was good and her husband was a nice gentleman. After that, we went for our dinner to a restaurant. Thereafter, we reached the station for our Bhavnagar train.

At 11 PM, we boarded the train for Bhavnagar. We reached Bhavnagar at about 5 AM and met my sister, brother-in-law and my little nephew. We visited the beautiful beach and palace in Bhavnagar. We stayed there for two nights and returned to Ahmadabad on Monday morning. We went to Uncle Wilson's apartment. We wanted to rest that day and then go to the old lady's house on Wednesday, as planned. But on that day, a telegram came from my mum and the message was asking me to not go to the girl's house. The one we visited unexpectedly on the first day.

We thought that my mum also wanted to see the girl and meet the family. My mum arrived at the Ahmadabad station and she approached Walter uncle furiously. She asked him why we visited so many girls in the city before going to Bhavnagar. We were all surprised seeing her behavior. Then, she showed us a telegram sent by the old lady to my mom, which said her son visited so many houses in Ahmadabad and it seemed to them that he will want to see many more girls before he decided to marry her grand-daughter. And that she didn't want me to come to her house. This was a shock for me, but the Lord was on the move for me!

I was wondering why she'd written that kind of a telegram. But the Lord wanted to stop me from going there. Out of the millions of houses in the big city of Ahmadabad, why did I have to go to that particular house on that unexpected day and unexpected location? I was surprised because we did not see any girl and had not visited any house either! But the old lady must have sent some spy after us to see where we were going. On that day, all the houses we visited had girls matching my age. Amazingly, my Lord was there and He stopped me from going to that house.

The next day, Uncle Wilson asked me to not worry and that he had a good old man, a friend, who would guide us to find a good girl. All the moves I did were according to God's plan, protecting me because of my single prayer.

On Wednesday, we went to a house with Uncle Daniel. He took us to a house to meet the parents of a girl. Unfortunately, there was no one there but an old granny and the father of the girl. He seemed so confused that he could not make out who the candidate was! We figured the man was mad because he behaved very weirdly. I thought this was not the house the Lord wanted for me. But Uncle Daniel came with us and said that because we'd turned up without notice, he was confused. We accepted that and accepted the appointment given by Uncle Daniel.

The girl was working in a village, which was about 100 miles from the city. The father then went on Thursday to pick-up the girl. It was a government job so she could not just leave the job. She had to take permission from the head of the department. This was not possible because the head office was about 40 miles away from the workplace, but fortunately, the head of the department came to the station without any notice and found the girl on duty. The girl was attending a patient who was about to give birth.

The father reached at the same time and met the daughter and the head of the department at the same time. The girl refused to go with the father at first, but the head—an elderly lady—persuaded her and asked her to go. This was also the Lord's doing that the head of the department came unexpectedly. The permission was instantly given in writing. The next day was Friday; they traveled to come to Ahmadabad and arrived the same evening.

The following day was the day we were supposed to go and meet the family. This time, my mum and another uncle accompanied us. We were six in the team, ready to go and see the girl. This was the first girl I went to see with all the arrangements. We were given a warm welcome and shortly after, the girl came with simple clothes, no make-up and served tea and snacks very politely to us. At that time, the father mentioned that that was his daughter that works in the village and she had just arrived the previous night. We saw the girl, had a good chat with the family and left the house.

On our way back, Daniel uncle came cycling behind us to ask what our opinion was. I said that my mum should decide and mom said she seemed like a very good girl and the family seemed very good, too. She said that she liked the proposal but the decision depended on her son. I accepted the proposal and Daniel uncle was very happy. He took our message to them, giving us an invitation for the evening, to arrange the wedding and rituals.

We went to the house in the evening at about 6 PM and for the first time, I met the girl and spoke to her for about ten minutes and asked her a series of questions. Then, we were both happy to get married. Western civilizations will not understand this kind of a meeting and a girl agreeing to marry without knowing the man. In eastern countries, we rely more on our elders and the Lord.

In the evening, when we were discussing the marriage arrangements, to our surprise, the lady from Surat, whom we had the first meeting with before going to Bhavnagar, came to meet us and took part in the arrangements. I was surprised to see her there. She then asked me if I remembered her. I replied affirmatively and asked her how come she was there. She said the girl I was marrying was her brother's daughter. She was immediate family. I smiled at her and she started a conversation with my mum—because she knew her too!

The ritual was performed and both parties agreed on a marriage date. I was supposed to return to my work in Africa so I wanted a quick marriage.

Our marriage was arranged for the 5th March 1966. Both parties started the arrangements. The invitation card was ready and mailed already but in the final week, I had four marriage offers from Bombay-based families and they all came through the priest of our church. The priest's wife asked me to consider the offers. My mum told her that my son would not change. I was all set for my marriage as arranged in Ahmadabad because it was a God-arranged match made in heaven and we were simply going to celebrate the wedding just to get our Lord's blessings.

Our Marriage (March 5, 1966)

It was a marriage of trust and faith—not meeting the girl and just trusting my family for an arranged marriage. I hardly met my wife-to-be for 10 minutes at the first meeting, and for about 15 minutes the day I was leaving Ahmadabad. We hardly spoke to each other; it was a very brief meeting. I trusted in the Lord and with absolute faith, we joined in matrimony.

For a boy to get married is to get nice clothing, a nice shirt, a necktie and suit, and to go with his family and friends and be guests of the bride's family. The bride's side had lots of work to do; they would have to make arrangements for the groom's party and food; decorating the church and many more small and big items to arrange for.

A day before the marriage, my side's marriage party—about 100 members of my family—took a train in the morning and reached Ahmadabad at 4.10 PM. We went straight to the bride's home. They entertained us well and, as arranged, the bride and groom's party members were getting ready for the engagement ceremony. The bride's-side members were more than 200 that were present at the ceremony. The priest of their church performed the ceremony. We exchanged the rings and exchanged the garlands as per the rituals in our culture. We were now engaged and the girl's family gave us some privacy. They gave us a room to speak to each other in. At that time, we hardly spoke to each other. I was 27 years old and she was 24 years old. We were fully mature but hardly knew each other.

On the eve of the marriage, there was a music party and celebration from the bride's side.

The next day was the wedding at the church.

I was sitting in the car which was decorated with fresh flowers. My mum was with me and so were some other elders from my immediate family. At that time, one very old woman—like my Grandma—with her fragile voice, came near my window. She put her hand on my head and blessed me. I still do not know what kind of blessings they were. I felt like my grandma's spirit was in her and she blessed me before going to church.

With a loud musical band, the marriage party walked towards the church. The church was about two miles through the Ahmadabad city.

We reached the church and all my relatives came and settled on the left side of the church' pews and the girl's side members settled on the right-side pews. Everyone was waiting for the bride to arrive. The bride arrived with her mother on one side and her father on the other. There was no music for the bride entering the church but the church choir started singing marriage-related hymns.

There were six priests and one bishop to bless the marriage. My mother had good standing with the church and our community. They respected her and all the priests were very friendly with our family. They all came and, one by one, took turns reading the Bible, prayers and other messages pertaining to the marriage ceremony. The bishop blessed us at the end of the ceremony. As per Indian culture, we exchanged garlands. I lifted up the veil of the bride but there is no kissing ritual in the eastern culture.

After the marriage, we walked out of the church and there, all our friends and family members honored us with garlands of fresh flowers. As the garlands became heavy, we took off some of the garlands and handed them over to the best man to ease our necks. After that, there were photographs taken with the families. When that was over, we were given a car to go to the photo studio to get a perfect marriage photo—which we still have in our house.

In all the ceremonies, the last one was at the house of the bride. As we entered the house, the people around us showered flowers on us. Musicians started playing music loudly with a trumpet, drums and keyboard, using loudspeakers. The singer was singing a song, which I still remember. It was a song similar to the song sung by Solomon in the Bible in the Songs of Solomon.

The song was: *Baharo Phool Barsawo*

"Oh beautiful nature, shower flowers; my beloved has come,"

"Oh sweet winds, blow sweet melody; my beloved has come,"

"The fragrance of henna is flowing towards me and the hands of my beloved are decorated"

"The beauty of the Lily made her face bright and red color of the flower is seen on her lips"

A similar song is in the Bible, in the 'Songs of Solomon', Chapter 4:16

"Awake, north wind; and come, south wind!"

Blow on my garden, that its fragrance may spread abroad,

Let my lover come into his garden and taste its choice fruits."

All that happened during our marriage was like blessings pouring on us from heaven.

We entered into the house and were given a marriage banquet. It was a simple meal with some sweets. It was a difficult thing for my in-law's family to feed more than 25 persons at home. The state's law was that no gathering should feed more than 25 persons because of a shortage of grain in the state. We knew the problems, so meals were served in two venues to make sure the police department did not come and cause trouble. The huge pots of food were kept in rickshaws, ready to take off in case of any police raid.

Anyway, the marriage was over and it was time to take leave from the in-law's family. Usually, the girl meets her parents before leaving their home for the last time and the weeping and hugging starts. At the end, I had to go and comfort the parents and give them assurance that she will be taken care of at our home. We left the house and came to the railway station. There, we spoke to each other freely and walked together and became a little free.

It was an overnight train to Bombay. We reached home at about 7 AM. All our neighbors came to meet us at the entrance of our home and they greeted my wife for the first time. The situation was such that the house was so small, that we did not have any privacy. After three days, I took my wife to show her around the city of Bombay. At that time, we were still strangers to each other.

After seven days of the marriage, we went on a honeymoon tour. We went to Delhi and Agra to see the Taj Mahal. We had a good time together and we became acquainted to each other. The 17th of March was her birthday; we went to a special restaurant for a nice meal. She was very happy to get such a celebration. The next day, we returned to Ahmadabad to meet her family. When we reached home, her neighbors and friends came to meet us. We had a very good time together at her home.

The Lord Answered My Prayer

The next day, her mother and her sisters asked me a question in private, about my visits to the other families prior to the marriage, when I was going to Bhavnagar to meet my eldest sister.

I laughed and said that I did not see any girl prior to the marriage and that my wife was the first girl I saw and agreed to marry. My mother-in-law told me that she heard that I had gone to see a girl in a house before going to Bhavnagar. I was shocked to hear what was cooking behind my back. My mother-in-law knew about the old granny whose granddaughter I was supposed to meet! I explained that I had gone to the granny's home by accident. Whether it was an accident or it was the plan of my Lord, God did not want me to marry that girl.

The granny was the headmistress of the school where my mother-in-law was a teacher. On that Saturday, when I went to see the girl whom I was supposed to marry, (my wife) my mother-in-law went to get permission from the school, for taking the day off. The headmistress asked who the boy was. She replied that the boy was from Africa the family from Bombay. She fumed and said, "Oh that boy! He is a playboy, and he has gone to every house in Ahmadabad."

My Mother-in-law told me this after the marriage. She said that she was very worried about agreeing to this marriage because she had heard about me from a second person—the first lady was the lady from Surat; the one who was Walter uncle's friend. The granny sent a spy to see where I was going and whom I was meeting. I did not go and see any girl on that day. I was just in transit to Bhavnagar to see my eldest sister. But all that happened according to my Lord. He took me to the house of His choice and I was married to the girl of His choice, the choice of my mum and of course, my choice—with blessings from above. These were the mysterious ways of how my Lord sent that lady that spied on me and brought me to the house of His choice.

My mother-in-law was very surprised and became very happy after my explanations. She told the old lady, the headmistress, about her misunderstanding. She repented and asked for forgiveness through my mother-in-law. It was too late. Every time I sent photos to my mother-in-law, she showed the photos to her and she grieved that it was a big mistake on her part.

Now, it was time to return to Africa. I was all set—my family from distant villages came to see me off. My grandma, (my mum's mother) asked my mum if her son was going back the next day. My mum told her that he was booked to return to his work. The same night, she died of heart failure. We rushed to see her at her house. It was nighttime; we went to look for a phone to call Walter uncle, granny's son, to inform him and other families about the sad news. At about 1 PM, we knocked on the door of a businessman and begged him for a call to Surat. He was very kind; he called Surat and passed the message to the night guard of the municipal office where Walter uncle was employed. We called and hoped that he would get the message. I decided to cancel my tickets and attend the funeral. In the morning, Walter uncle came, uninformed, to see me off to Africa. He was stunned to find his mother dead. It was a very sad moment for all of us. I went to the airline office and extended my stay in Bombay. I had one more week with my newly-wedded wife and my family. The week was sad, and I returned in sadness to Africa.

Back to Work

When I returned to Lusaka, I found that Augustine had done a good job taking care of the business. He did not buy any commodities but had accumulated some money in the bank. We lived with a family so we did not have the problem of evening meals. At lunchtime, however, we had our cook who was sickly and could not work much but was happy to prepare very tasty food for us. Augustine used to give him the menu and we enjoyed his food every day. We were waiting for my wife to come so that we could have a family life.

We had problems living on our own. So, we found a friend who kept us with him and his wife cooked very good food. Mr. Parshottam Divecha, an electrician, had a small house but his heart was big. He kept us with him and took care of us. Divecha's daughter now lives in Philadelphia; she is like my daughter. She is married to a fine gentleman named Deepak, who is a CPA and doing well. They are both very helpful to me when I have big occasions in my family; they take part like one of our own. Thereafter, I found another friend who had a bigger house, offering me a room. He was Mr. Chhagan Waghela; he was like my elder brother. His wife Manju-*ben* was like my own sister. They were very helpful to me. They took good care of me. They are now in Dallas. God separated me from my brothers and sisters but did not keep me lonely.

My Business in Lusaka

We were getting very busy at our shop. Business was flourishing, Augustine used to take trips to the city for buying goods for the business and for banking and paying bills. So, I concentrated fully on my business. In all that busy time, I received a message from India that my wife was pregnant. This was our happiest moment. We were both looking forward for my wife to come and settle down in our family life, because we were depending on others to take care of our daily life. We were like gypsies moving from one place to the other. Finally, I rented a good house in the middle of the city.

We moved into the house and expected my wife to get her passport and her resident permit to join me. I started working on it. Finally, the British Embassy gave her a passport to travel to Lusaka, Zambia. When my wife, Priscilla, travelled to Zambia I was waiting for her at the Lusaka airport, but message came that the flight had halted at Ndola.

My dad asked her to cancel the further journey and enter Ndola city. She was shy and could not talk to my dad much. She did exactly what he said. I had to take a train to Lusaka to pick her up.

It was convenient because I was supposed to pick up a van, which I'd bought and paid for. It was ready to be picked up. It was an Opel van, which I needed to carry my shop's goods. From Ndola, Priscilla and I started our journey in the afternoon, through the jungles of Africa.

Priscilla was stunned looking at the jungle and how no people were seen on the way. It was a new experience for her because she came from a crowded city in India. There, on the long 430-mile journey, there was not a single soul. She was scared and kept looking around the jungle. Occasionally, some car or truck passed by. We reached Lusaka at about 7 PM—that's when the city's lights were seen from afar.

When we reached Lusaka city, I did not take her home but took her around the city to show her that the place was full of people and there were shops and cars running on the road. She felt relieved and started speaking with me with joy. After that, we went home where Augustine was eagerly waiting for us. He met his sister-in-law for the first time. We considered him our son.

The kitchen, and the whole environment, was different for her. The next day, we went shopping for kitchen utensils and some groceries to set up our kitchen. By God's grace, she'd reached Africa safely. She was pregnant and kept good health. After all, she was a trained WHO (World Health Organization)-certified nurse and Health Visitor.

In Lusaka, she wanted to join the hospital but I needed her more for my business. Now that we'd become a family of three, we used to go to the shop and work till late. She became the cashier in my shop and we were attending to the customers. My wife was pregnant and we were expecting our first baby. It was a different feeling; I did not know anything about what a pregnant wife would want. But we had good neighbors and good friends in Lusaka.

One such good friend was Mr. Parshottam Divecha and his wife Ratanben, who used to call me her brother. She took charge of Priscilla during the pregnancy. When our son George was born, Ratanben came with me to the hospital and took my wife and our new-born son, George, to her house and kept them there for a good one month, nursing my wife and the baby to health. I can never thank her enough for all that she has done for us.

When George was born, my father came from Ndola to see the baby and Priscilla. My mum came after a year to see my son. We were a very happy family, by the grace of our Lord.

Through Our Son George (Tiku), the Grace of God Poured in Our Life

The day George was born, we were overwhelmed. I saw that my wife and son were both in good health. I ran to the post office to send telegrams to my mother and in-laws. They received the telegrams and wrote letters congratulating us.

When George was only seven months old, he had diarrhea. So, we took him to our primary care doctor. The doctor prescribed some medication to stop the diarrhea. It did not stop but only got worse. The doctor suggested taking him to the hospital. We took him to the hospital and George was admitted in a special room. He was in Lusaka Hospital for 10 days, in isolation. We were not allowed to go near him. We used to look at him from the window. We used to sit there till late night. The doctors at the hospital gave up hope of curing his disease. We were worried about him. All medication failed; we could not give him milk so we kept him on glucose water. We prayed for him and waited for some miracle to happen.

During the weekend, my dad came to see him and he was also very worried. On Sunday evening, as dad was about to leave for the airport, he stopped and asked us to let him try his medication. This medication was naturopathy (herbal), which helps and does no harm, even if you take large dosages. It is called the "Mother of medicine" in India. He asked for Himaj-Harde powder, which we had in our house. He took half a glass of water and mixed Himaj-Harde in it. Himaj-Harde is used for cleaning the stomach by inducing loose motions. I told him that that would make his diarrhea worse.

He mixed the medication well in water and told my wife to give him two or three spoons of Himaj-Harde water. She gave the solution with much worry. George was in her hand. In five minutes, George had loose motion. We were worried. My dad was also very worried. We waited to see what would happen.

Halleluiah! After that, George did not pass any motion for three days. We gave him milk and he was cured. He showed brightness in his eyes. All our sleepless nights and worries were gone. My wife used to take care of him during daytime and I used to take turns at night. We both had lots of worries but, praise the Lord, George was cured completely. This was our Lord's doing. This is the miracle of prayer.

In Francistown, Botswana, when George was three years old, he got lost. My wife looked for him, shouting his name, but he was not to be found. Irene and I ran around the neighborhood to find him. We did not find him. At last, when my wife started crying, he giggled slightly—we found him sitting under our bed. He had strips of soluble Aspirin in his hand, which he was slowly chewing on. It was sweet so he had eaten about three of them. We took him in our arms because he was smiling while looking at us. We rushed him to a doctor and had him checked. The doctor confirmed that he had not had much because the silver foil was strong. Praise the Lord, for he was well. From that day, we kept all our medication locked up.

On one Saturday, when we were shopping, we entered a friend's shop which was empty. The owner was my good friend. George was, as usual, running up and down the shop's floor. It was hard, cement flooring. He slipped on the floor and fell on his head. He went into a coma for a few seconds. We picked him up and threw some water on him to revive him. He was fine but we were worried about him and took him to the doctor. The doctor checked him thoroughly and asked us to watch him for a few days. We kept him in our arms for a few days. We kept him between us in bed, at night, and kept an eye on him. He was sleeping well and showed no adverse signs. We had to keep him on a leash when we went shopping. He was full of mischief and very strong.

In Botswana, the school segregated him because of the South African color discrimination policy. He was neglected during school sports. In his first grade, he had a good teacher but in the second grade, he was neglected and I had problems with the headmaster. He was not given a chance to participate in any sport; he was pushed aside. I was very furious but still, I did not say anything. At the parents-teachers meetings, four of us parents asked questions about the segregation and had a good fight with the administration but they still did not pay us any heed. It was the South African segregation policy that was still in effect in Botswana.

My dad asked me why I didn't send him to India. I thought India would lay a good foundation for our son. We sent him to India. He was in one of the best schools in India, in a hill station named Panchgani.

When he was in the 8ᵗʰ class, I went to see the school with my wife. I was shocked to see the condition of his bedsheet—patched; shoes—patched and I didn't like it. I discussed with the lady caretaker about the bad living conditions of my son. She showed no concern. I decided to take him back to Africa. Times had changed and George had a good education in India. His foundation was strong.

The same year, I sent round-trip tickets for George to visit us in Africa. My dad was not happy sending him because he was about to complete his high school the following year. I had to send round-trip tickets to show that I would be sending him back after his vacation. My dad wrote to me saying that I was going to spoil his education and that he will not be sending George to Africa.

I read the letter and thought George was not coming. We started our journey to South Africa. We were in a hotel in Johannesburg, thinking about our son. I was telling my wife that if George had traveled today, he would have been at the Johannesburg airport. My wife suggested that we inquire the Johannesburg airport authorities about our son. Maybe, he was at the airport. I called the airport from the hotel. British Airways said that he was there, waiting to board the Botswana Airlines flight. I told the air hostess to hold him there itself because we were in Johannesburg and that we would come and pick him up soon.

I drove very fast because the British Airways staff may not keep him and may put him on the Botswana flight. We reached the airport and the air hostess brought him out. We were so happy that our son was with us. We took him with us on our tour to Durban. We really enjoyed the tour because all three of our children were together and had a good time.

We did not send our son back to India. He stayed with us in Botswana. I took him to Plumtree High school, Plumtree, Zimbabwe, for his 9ᵗʰ-grade admission. The principal spoke with him and asked him some questions. George replied to all the questions but his Indian accent was not acceptable. The headmaster said that the school's standard was much higher and that he could not take our son because his standard was lower than their standard. The headmaster refused his admission. I argued and told him that his academic standard was higher than their students' in the 9ᵗʰ grade. The principal then said that he will test him. I agreed. George did very well at his test and the principal agreed to admit him. But he was placed in 9ᵗʰ 'C' class. The 'A' class's students were highly talented. George gave his first test after three months and his score was much higher than the average of his class. The teacher decided to upgrade George to the 'A' class. Then, George had tough competition. He was given a separate room for his studies. He worked hard. In the first test in the 'A' class, he was not the topper but was still in the top five.

George was very good in sports. He played hockey, was a swimmer and an athlete. We used to attend his sports events and were very proud of our son. George completed his Cambridge "O" level and "A" level certification and we brought him to the USA for a tougher level of education.

I am proud to write that though George went through a hard time in his school and college days, he achieved his goal and he graduated from Missouri Medical College as a Doctor.

By the time of his doctorate studies, he came to India, while we were there, for one month medical course in India. During that time we arranged his marriage. It was difficult to select his life partner, because he was born in Africa, lived in America and India was like his foreign country. We visited couple families and we selected a girl from Gandhinager city near Ahmadabad, but it was not confirmed. We gave our son little time to think about it. After few months George confirmed the girl name Teena, while we were in Africa. We arranged the marriage over the phone with Teena's parents, Mr. Irwinbhai and Shashiben, the Baraiya family. George returned to India for the marriage. With the blessings of our Lord, the marriage was arranged and date was fixed. George took frequent trips to Gandhinager to meet Teena and the family. Both Teena and George were now confirmed, and we arranged formalities of the marriage. For us the formalities were unique, and the marriage was celebrated exotically. George and Teena went to Singapore for the honeymoon and returned after about a week. After that George returned back to his college and concentrated on his studies. After sometime going through the immigration formalities, Teena arrived in America and settled in the small town of Missouri, which was for her a painful experience, because she came from a big and much crowded city. But George and Teena lived happily.

He studied further and became a physician in Internal Medicine from Chicago and from Detroit, Michigan he achieved his final goal—he became a Gastroenterologist.

George and Teena have a talented son name Nolen is now ten years old. George and Teena are now running a clinic at Tennessee, (USA).

Lusaka

We were members of the Trinity Church of Lusaka. I performed my duties as a steward and took active part in the church's activities. I was the only Indian Christian attending the Trinity Church. Every year, the Lord blessed us. He prospered us.

In any business, you get varieties of problems—mainly financial problems, in the payment of bills. Whenever I had a hitch, my Lord stood by me. I remember that, twice, when I had problems with huge payments, I went to see the bank manager. Amazingly, the manager said that my payment had gone through because some customers credited my business account by telegraphic transfer. Coming out of the bank, sitting in the car, I used to thank God for the help because I thought I will have to ask the manager to give me an overdraft but I did not have trouble at any time. All my troubles were taken care of supernaturally.

Then, the time came when I thought that we are three in the shop and could do something else. I thought of opening a clothing distribution channel, importing goods from overseas and selling it to the local buyers.

But at this point, Augustine mentioned that he wished to study further. I was happy to hear that he wanted to study more. I had no opportunities to study further. So, I thought why not I give an opportunity to my little brother. I asked him what he wanted to do. He had some young Indian friends who were going to Evelyn Hone College for Electronic Engineer's studies. The course offered at the college was the "City of Guild of London"—a telecommunications technician course. It was the best course for my little brother because he had nine surgeries during his childhood. God was making plans for us. I asked my brother to go to the college and get himself enrolled. The course was expensive but we could afford it. I was very happy that my brother was going to do his studies. He went to the college with his friends and filled in forms for the course but he was rejected because his English was not good. In the evening, he came to the shop frustrated and crying. I patted him and told him not to worry, and that I would go and see the principal.

The next day, I went to see the principal, leaving him and my wife at the shop. I asked the principal about the course and the requirements for it. My brother fulfilled the all requirements for the course, but only his language was the problem. I explained to the principal about our background, ailments and disabilities of my brother. The principal agreed to admit him and said that he we will see his progress and review it in six months' time. My brother worked hard and passed the first test with good marks. The principal accepted him for the course. Augustine achieved his goal in four years' studies and passed his examination of 'City and Guild' of London. He received a certificate with a contract of practical work with a local telephone company. One day, he came home and said that he had installed lots of telephones in the new international hotel, all by himself. My wife and I went to the hotel to see his work. We had our evening meal at the hotel and saw one of the rooms he'd installed the phone in. We were thrilled to see that he had good confidence in his work. When the three-month contract was over, he looked for a job. A television sales company, for repairing radios and black and white televisions, employed him. There were no color televisions at that time. In a short time, he did good work at the shop. When I went to visit the owner of the shop, he praised his work. The company gave him a permanent job.

I bought a residential plot in Lusaka, near the Evelyn College, on the road where the Fire Station of Lusaka was situated—Makishi road. I hired a builder on a contract to build a semi-detached house—two houses with one common wall. We were preparing to move in by the month of June but my Lord did not want us to settle there. God wanted to move me to Botswana. Due to the political situation, we could not move into our own house. So, we rented it to an international company.

The Farm in Lusaka

I believe that I had a curse—that all the houses I bought or built, I could not live in. I had several houses, but I could not make any of them my home. Many people said that it's just bad luck but I do not believe that, knowing the bible verse: *Unless the Lord builds the house, its builders labor in vain.* In Botswana, I bought a house on Priscilla's shoe company's name and we lived in it for a long time very comfortably.

I bought a 20-acre farm in Lusaka, Zambia, on Augustine's name. But we had to leave Zambia for political reasons. The farm was abandoned because there was a danger of attacks from political members. They were attacking foreigners in their farms. Some of them were killed. I was not a citizen so I had to be cautious.

The farm was in a very good agricultural area. It was very close to the city. It had a borehole and fertile soil. It was a developed farm; it was previously owned by a farmer who died. His widow, Mrs. Lybwarch, could not live alone so she sold it to me and left Zambia to live in Salisbury (now Harare).

I was in similar jeopardy. After leaving Zambia, I took several trips to Lusaka and found that the farm was still empty, but I could not do anything about it because of the law that the absentee landlord loses the land.

Our Two Daughters

Angelina: Blessed Angel, With a New Life in Botswana

Angelina was born when I started my hat factory in Botswana. Business had picked up by exporting goods to the neighboring countries. I was comfortable exporting goods. I'd established my house and had a good name in business. I went to Lusaka to see Angelina and I saw my baby for the first time. Nelson and Augustine were there in our house. At that time, fortunately, our Lord moved for us and my sister-in-law Bhanuben visited us and was of good help to my wife. I closed my factory for three weeks for Christmas holidays.

I was accompanied by a friend—a Medical Doctor who was originally from Peshawar but married to a lady in London and had served in Tristan De Cunha Island as a British Doctor—and I found him a job in Botswana. I wanted to have company driving through the jungle of Kalahari Desert. He accompanied me because he wanted to see Zambia. He stayed for a week and returned by air.

I took my wife, George and the newborn, Angelina, and travelled 1400 miles to Botswana. It was a pleasant trip. Angelina and George played happily together. George was very happy with his sister; he often kept asking when his sister was going to walk, as he wanted someone to play with.

Angelina did her primary education in Francistown and she did her high school in Bulawayo, Zimbabwe. She is now a qualified Doctor of Pharmacy, graduated from the medical college of San Francisco.

Angelina is married to Sanjay and has three children—Nicholas, Sarah and Stephen.

Sylvia—the Angel born in our house

When Sylvia was born, my mother-in-law Katherine, and sister-in-law Edna (Manorama) visited us. We did not have problems when Sylvia was born. At that time, we were in Botswana and I was very busy with my work. Priscilla was very happy with her mother and sister visiting us.

On the evening of 27th November, we all went to the hospital at the time Sylvia was supposed to be born. We waited till 11 PM and saw that Priscilla was comfortable. The nurses told us to go home and that she would call us when the baby arrived.

Priscilla went into labor late at night; she was given a cowbell to ring. My wife rang the bell several times but the nurses were busy chatting. In the process, the cowbell's pendulum dropped out of the bell. Pricilla was in panic because the nurses were in the general ward. She was in the private ward, in the labor room. Priscilla had to bang the bell on one side of the bed, which was an iron bar. Fortunately, the nurses heard the bang and came running.

Sylvia was born. The hospital was like a small clinic where the nurses were careless. It was a small town-clinic with no modern facilities. I got a call at about 1.30 AM when we'd just fallen asleep. As soon as we heard about the birth of a girl, we rushed to the hospital. In the process, as I was sleepy, I reversed my car and accidentally banged it on a big rock which was outside the house gate. I was fully awake then and drove slowly to the hospital, which was only ten minutes away from the house. We reached the hospital and saw that my wife was in good health and Sylvia was sleeping by her.

Sylvia did her high school education in Bulawayo, Zimbabwe. After passing her high school, Cambridge "O" level, she moved to the USA for further education.

Sylvia graduated as a DMD—Dental degree from Philadelphia. Immediately after that, she married Samir. They have two daughters, Nicole (Anjali) and Isabelle (Emma).

We are proud parents because our children are doctorate degree holders and are doing well. It all happened to us because God was and is gracious to us. We were constantly praying.

The Lord's Master Plan: Bitter to Sweet—Like Honey

In 1968, the President of Zambia announced that 31 key companies had been nationalized overnight and that all the rural shops were to be nationalized at the end of the year. My shop was affected and I had to start winding up my business. I was out of job by the end of 1968.

The shop was closed after good Christmas business. I thought that it was the end of my business career, but my Lord had some other plan for me. I surrendered myself to the Lord for my future. There, I surrendered myself to the Lord in my prayers. The Lord opened another avenue for me. He gave me the ability to go and become a salesman. Instead of customers coming to me like in a retail shop, I had to go to the customers and sell commodities in quantities and earn sales commissions. I had a vehicle and I had the courage to go ahead as per the plan of my Lord.

Amazing changes happened to me in my business life; I was getting successful responses. I gained self-confidence and expanded working from Lusaka to Livingstone—an area about 300 miles away, on partly rough roads, stopping in every big town, selling various commodities to the customers.

I was given feedback by my suppliers that some customers were good and that they were buying in big quantities and that none of the previous salespersons were successful in those companies. I liked the challenging work. I was determined to go to the most difficult buyers and see what I faced. At one place, I had to encounter an old lady who was a very odd kind of a person to even approach. I took a chance and went to her in the morning, at 9 AM. All businesses opened at 8 AM in Zambia. So, I allowed them to open the shop and get settled for the day. I went there and asked for the buyer of the organization. Instead of inviting me into her office, she came out and, without any greetings, asked me who I was, rudely. I introduced myself to her and handed over my business card. She asked me why she should buy from me. I said I had come to her in good faith. She asked why. She told me that no one from my company came to her and that she had not seen anyone for a long time! Obviously, she knew my company.

I replied saying that I was confident and that I was not going from there empty-handed. I added that I did not know about others but she was such a kind person she came from her office to meet me and that I felt honored. She was softening down and asked me to come to her office.

Then, she asked me if I wanted to drink tea. I said that if it was masala tea, I would appreciate it because I got watery tea at the hotel. She was so happy that she offered me to come and stay at her house whenever I came to the city. She said that I didn't have to make appointments and could just pop in at any time. I was so thankful to the Lord for helping me in breaking through this difficult person. After teatime, she gave me the biggest order of the trip. The suppliers could not believe that I'd taken such a big order.

God was with me all the time because I was successful, not in my own strength but by God's grace. He gave me these abilities. I was successful but it was not enough for me because I saw no future in this kind of business—traveling long distances.

I was looking for something good and something permanent. After about seven months of traveling, the Zimbabwe director of my dad's company, Mr. Gershman, approached me. I was surprised to see such a gesture! He asked me to start a hat factory for them in Botswana. I was given work as the manager of the company. I was not very sure about the future of my life in the textiles industry. Mr. Gershman must have noticed my abilities and my salesmanship. After all, I was selling his goods.

I was not very happy to leave Zambia, but I was persuaded by the director of my dad's company, who asked me to visit him. I went to visit him in Botswana. This came to me when I was in search of some job opening. The Lord moved me to accept the job in Botswana.

I was given an opportunity to go to the undeveloped country to develop my future. I went to Botswana to see what it looked like. The country was in a primitive stage. It was a newly-independent country. The little town I visited was called Francistown—a small commercial town of Botswana. The town had only one street and a small primitive train station and a post office. There was a hotel in a primitive stage with village-type round buildings with thatched roofs, but spacious rooms. That was the best hotel in town.

Looking at the primitive place, I was not very happy but the country did not have any political problems. The currency used was the South African Rand. I saw the little town and I was disheartened. Unhappy I was put in small town, the company's main director asked me to go to Johannesburg. I went to Johannesburg, South Africa, to see a hat factory. I was supposed to stay in Johannesburg and learn to make hats. I left Zambia for a new chapter of my life.

I entered Botswana on September 29, 1969, and achieved much success— our daughter Angelina was born a year after. She brought upon us entirely new blessings.

Life in Botswana Began

I was staying at the Grand Hotel and eating at the restaurant. I was not very happy because I did not like the western kind of food much. In that small town, I found good friends. They were Amina and Muhammad Jasat. Amina was very friendly and she called me her brother. Muhammad was from India and Amina was born in Zimbabwe. God sent help to me, somehow, in that strange place and in a strange way. He provided good food and good friends. I was never hungry. God took good care of Elijah when he had no food; The Lord provided for my needs.

I went to Johannesburg for training for seven days. Johannesburg is a big city with congested traffic and a variety of people. When I reached Johannesburg for the first time, the manager of South Africa came to meet me at the airport. I was supposed to have taken smallpox vaccination health documents, but it was not known to me. I was held-up at the immigration but Mr. Booty Sole, a Jewish man—the manager of our South African Branch—came in and promised to get me the smallpox shot the same day, in the city. Mr. Sole was very fluent in the Afrikaans language. He convinced the officers in his executive style.

They trusted him and let me go. South Africa was not good for non-whites. I had no idea about how officers behaved with non-whites. I went to the city and found no place for me to stay. I was taken to the Indian area—the Ford's burg and Mayfair areas—and there, an Indian hotel's owner gave me accommodation. He gave me the best room, as I was a stranger from India. He took good care of me and gave me good breakfast in my room. I was happy to be among my own people.

The next day, Mr. Booty Sole picked me up and took me to the hat factory. We met in the entrance to the cabin of the main director, Mr. Simon Pozniak. He saw that I was an Indian; he did not seem very happy. I could see his odd behavior but later found out that he was not discriminative.

Simon did not allow me to enter the factory area. The owners were Jewish. The elder brother was the general manager and the little brother was the technical manager taking care of the technical work of the factory. I was not allowed because they said that the Indian man might learn their trade and open a factory against them. In the world, most businesses are run by the Jewish and if the Jewish failed, the Indians would be the ones to take over the business.

The Zimbabwe directors had a long talk with him over the phone and finally, he agreed to let me enter the factory just to see and not to do any physical work. I was happy with that. I walked in with the factory manager, Mr. Delaqua—an Italian gentleman. His wife was also working at the factory as a supervisor. They were very kind to me and showed all the machines and their connections and the layout of the factory. I had a small pocket diary where I jotted down all that I had seen the whole layout of the factory; I made diagrams so I could use the same in my factory.

After seven days, I returned to Francistown. I was received very warmly by one of the Zimbabwe directors, right at the airplane's door. He handed over to me the keys to a Land Rover. I was now mobile and I stayed at the Grand Hotel—the only good hotel in the town. Fortunately, it was Botswana's long holiday weekend. I took good rest on that day.

The next day was Botswana's Independence Day. I drove up to the celebration ground. It was a very dusty place and the wind blew very heavily. The tent where the guests were sitting was shaking. The celebration was in the open ground. I was sitting in my Land Rover, looking at the passing out parade and other local dances.

It was a holiday for Independence Day. I had no work on that day, so, after the Independence celebration, I went to see what kind of machines I had and what raw materials arrived for me to start the hat factory. I was told, over the phone, that the technical manager from Johannesburg would be delayed. He said that he might come after four weeks, to set up the factory for me. I waited for him for two days but he was not promising. He wanted me to wait for about a month or more. I was not happy with the situation.

I went into town looking for a plumber or a mechanic. I found a motor mechanic. I would say he was a roadside mechanic with good skills of welding and plumbing. He wanted a job because his garage was not doing well.

He came with me and I showed him his work and the layout describing how to connect the machines and install a boiler and provide connections to the hat machines.

Praise the Lord, with his good help and that of help of some other helpers, we managed to set up the factory. We asked the town engineer to give us a temporary electrical connection. He was very helpful to us. This was the first privately-owned factory in town. Everyone was excited seeing the new development in town. The factory was in the newly-allocated industrial area. Even power connection was not available yet.

I want to mention with much honor the name of the town engineer, Mr. Mike Ives. He was a very kind gentleman. Though he was from South Africa, he was not discriminative. He gave us a temporary connection, running the cable on the ground. We connected the boiler to the hat-molding machines which worked on steam. Mie was an expert on the steam boilers so he helped to start the boiler and connected to the hat-molding machine. Mike was a great help.

The factory was ready in three days' time and I employed local workers to start work—to make hats. I had lots of raw material dumped in our warehouse. The first day, we made only 7 hats. They turned out good. The next day, we made about 20 hats. We were at full production in one week.

The following week, we exported the hats to Zambia—to my dad's company. I did not inform the Zimbabwe or South African companies that I'd managed to start my factory. I made an invoice and dispatch documents and exported 50 dozen hats in a two-week period. I sent a copy to the offices in Zimbabwe and South Africa, to give them a surprise.

There were no fax machines but I could send communication by a Telex machine. When they received my Invoices and my sales figures, the South African directors and Zimbabwe directors called me over the phone. They thought that I had dispatched raw hats. I told them to come and see my production. Both South African and Zimbabwe directors came rushing to my factory and were amazed to see my factory's layout and production.

"How did you manage this?" was the first question the South African technical director asked. I told him that he did not have time to come, so I managed to do it on my own. Immediately, the South African Director mentioned that he was not surprised as I was an Indian businessman and had copied his factory's operations without even touching any machinery. He told the Zimbabwe directors that that was why he was reluctant to allow me in his factory—because Indians were too quick to learn the trade. I told him that if he thought I would take business away from him, I was prepared to resign and promise that I would not start a hat factory anywhere in Africa. They were so happy to see my progress. My Lord gave me all this. I was nothing; He made me what I was.

At that time, the hat factory was the first private sector industry in Francistown and I was the first Indian expatriate to enter Botswana. I was allowed a Botswana entry permit because they thought that I was a British man—because my name was English and I had a British passport. But when I arrived in the country, they found out I was an Indian having British Passport, with a western name. They did not allow Indians in Bechuanaland, but after it became independent, it became Botswana and I was accepted as the first Indian immigrant. Therefore, I became the first Indian Christian to enter Botswana. I became a pioneer of the industry.

I started 10 different industries in Botswana: two distribution companies and four shops. My wife managed all the shops. The shops were: a shoe shop, a sports shop which was taken over from Bata Shoe Company, a toys shop, and a restaurant. My cousins, Ivor and Edward, furnished the restaurant during my absence from the city.

I faced a lot of persecution from the South African white population, but I was not into politics—I was a simple businessman. There was a club where only whites were allowed. I did not care that they did not allow me in their club. It was called Francistown Club but people called it a 'White Club.' The segregation was obvious because of South African influence but I did not cross any barrier where I was not accepted.

One day, Mr. Jack Male, the Manager of the Standard Chartered Bank came to my office. I used to help him with customs clearing and his bank money transfers from Botswana to their branch in Kasane, through Zimbabwe. I used to custom clear the documents for him and never charged any money for the services I gave him. The manager asked me to come to the club saying that and he would sign the petition for me and get 10 other club members to sign the application. I told him that I did not go where I was not accepted. They were uneducated and labor-class people, and I did not want to be discriminated against by them. I'd rather live with my Church friends and other business friends. I did not drink liquor or smoke; I did not dance; I did not even play the games they played at the club. So, there was no point in me joining the club. Mr. Jack Male, an old man, and his wife were very sad that I did not go to the club because of the segregation. The club changed their policy in a few years but I still did not join the club. Jack Male and his wife offered me come to their house and take books from their home library. The manager gave unlimited credit for my company.

On 23 September 1970, my second child, Angelina, was born. I could not leave my business and go to see my baby and my wife. I did not see my daughter for about three months but in December, during the Christmas holidays, I closed the factory and went to Zambia to see my wife and newborn—my little daughter, Angelina.

I had such good standing in the Botswana community that after a few years, the Home Minister met me at the town council office and asked me if he could regard me as a citizen of Botswana now. I replied in the negative because I did not want to give up my British Passport but I could not say that to him. He was concerned and asked why. I said that I didn't know that I could get citizenship. He told me that I was a citizen from that day onwards. He asked me to go and fill out forms and said that he would process my citizenship. Without any difficulty, I became a citizen of Botswana.

In 1973, I was on the board of directors of the company. I took charge of the company. At that time, the directors decided to start another factory in the same complex, next to the hat factory. We decided to start a ladies handbag factory.

I had to fly to Johannesburg to see a factory manufacturing the handbags. The factory's owner had ¼ stake in our investments. He offered to give machinery and supply us with material. He also promised that he would send personnel to visit our factory to improve our factory's production.

I went again to the same hotel in Ford's burg, the Indian area. Every day, a driver used to give me a ride to the handbag factory. I saw the various areas of the factory. I had no idea about making handbags. It was amazing to see over a thousand workers in that huge factory. The designing and cutting department was challenging for me. I walked around the factory and asked several questions to the supervisors in various departments. As usual, I wrote down what I needed to remember.

The machines were simple sewing machines but three machines were new for me. One was the skiving machine. The second was a plastic-heating and clicking machine and the third was the most important—a band-saw paper and board cutting machine. I studied those machines very carefully. In seven days, I was done with my tour of the factory and went to see the manager, Mr. Delaney.

He remarked in sarcasm, saying I was then a qualified bag maker. I replied that I was fully confident and did not need any help or even his expertise. He laughed and asked me if I could start the factory on my own. I replied affirmatively.

He did not believe me. When I reached Francistown, the machines had already arrived and some raw material was there. I went through each machine, lubricated it and trial-started it but they were all out of adjustment. I realized that someone had purposely done this to me—so that I'd have to call them for help.

I worked during the weekends and adjusted all the machines. I battled working on the skiving and plastic-laminating machines. But the following week, I was ready to start.

I employed 15 laborers to start the factory. The important workers were sewing machine operators. My Lord helped me; I had just the right workers for the sewing machines. The important machine was the walking-foot machine, which sewed the gusset to the body on both sides of the bags. I had two elderly semi-skilled ladies who performed the work perfectly. This was the Lord's blessing.

In the beginning, we had some teething problems but in two weeks' time, we could operate at our full production capacity. In one month, we started our full production and started exporting. This was a slap on Mr. Delaney's face. He came to see the factory with his production manager to check on my production.

My products were perfect but there was a need for more accurate work. I was not only successful in operating the factory but I also designed my own bags. The bags I designed were so good that they picked up big sales. Zambia and Malawi were demanding more. Mr. Delaney was confused and copied my designs. His factory had better sales in South Africa. One of the bags was made of suede cloth with fringes on one side. The fringe-design was new in the market and our sales were boosted. So did the South African companies'.

God works in mysterious ways in our life. I have experienced this on every step of my life. In ten months, the Zimbabwe and South African directors came with another idea to me—that they wanted to start a lace and trimmings-making factory. I was wondering how trimmings were made but they brought the machines and an expert from Austria. My work was to take care of the sales, make documents for the exports, pay the workers every weekend and make monthly payments to the manager. I did not have the responsibility of the production or the quality of the product.

The factory was working well but the Austrian manager resigned and went to work in a South African company for a bigger city with better prospects for him. We employed another Austrian manager but in two years' time, he was caught stealing. The board of directors wanted to put him in prison but I did not allow that because he had a wife and three children. I had problems running the factory at that time. I brought my cousin from India. Ivor and my maternal uncle, Ellison, came to Botswana.

I applied for their permits and found employment for them. The uncle was an electrician with practical skills but he did not have the skills of reading building-designs. He did not have English knowledge but my businessman-friend employed him with good wages and gave him a house and a car to drive. Ellison uncle had no knowledge of driving so he employed a driver to teach him driving. We did all that for him, but he was found not being productive in his work. He wanted to work the way he did in India. In six months, the owner of the company came to me and told me that he could not keep my uncle because he was not productive. I had another problem. I had to find a job for him but with his attitude and lack of knowledge of the English language, it was not possible. I organized a company for him and registered it for him. I got him a work permit and resident permit to work on his own. Now, he was supposed to go around and find piecework. My company gave him jobs and other Indian businessmen gave him some work so he could live on his own. I found a condo and asked him to take care of his own work and pay the house's rent and utilities. On the weekends, however, both Ivor and the uncle ate at my house. My wife used to make special exotic food for them.

Ivor was hard-working and enthusiastic to learn. He also had knowledge of the lathe machine, because he worked in India as a mechanic, earning very little wages. When he came to Botswana, I employed him at my lace and trimming factory because the manager was fired for stealing. There was no one to take care of the machine. I employed Ivor as the manager of the factory. His salary was good and he was well settled in a few months' time. He not only learned the machine work but also used to make parts for the machines and repaired them. I had no problems but he was not an effective manager. He could not command the workers and production was hampered. There was some stealing of laces and night-shift workers were found sleeping. I had to close the factory and employ my cousin in my factory. At that time, I started manufacturing T-shirts so I put him in the production floor. He worked under me but his wages were not good. I was not very happy but I wanted the factory to increase production so that I could give him better wages. The orders were not coming in and raw material did not come on time; most of the time, the factory did not have jobs. Just for Ivor, I kept the industry going and waited for new developments.

I went to Johannesburg to meet the directors to develop the T-shirt industry and prepared the strategy for the whole year. We went to meet the chain of group buyers and successfully took some orders for the next six months. Everything was ready and we were celebrating the day with a party in a hotel. Then, a phone call came from Francistown that the hat factory, bag factory and T-shirt machines were on fire. This was the biggest fire in Francistown, ever. The fire department did not have an idea as to how to put the fire out. It was a new experience for them. We could not believe that this could happen to us at the last moment. The party became the saddest moment for us. The next day, I flew to Francistown. It was during the Christmas holidays so there were no workers in the factory. Our neighbor was welding some pipes and the spark turned into a big fire, burning most of my factory. That was the end of my Hat factory. Ivor was out of a job.

I did not have my office or my factory, but my Lord was great. I went to my tobacco distribution industry office and worked from there. Ivor was out of work but I gave him a job at my shoe shop, which my wife was running as a retail business. The problem was that I could not pay Ivor more than the pay I used to give him at the lace factory.

In Botswana, I established 12 different industries, including:

Everest Mills (Pty) Ltd. Manufacturing knitted fabric of man-made fiber.

For the same company, I started another company named

Shashi Textiles (Pty) Ltd, a weaving mill weaving suiting fabric.

We had to build the factory with special specifications as required for a weaving mill. The building plans had specifications, which were done under my supervision. After that, we bought 42 double-shuttle looms from a weaving machine company in Rutti, Switzerland. We employed a special loom tuner named Mr. Hans Fischer to train local workers. Everest Mills and Shashi Textile Mills are still a big manufacturing company, weaving indigo cloth and blankets. This is the biggest workplace in Botswana, which is still employing over 1000 workers.

Resigned from Work

I was sleeping in my bedroom; it was about 2 AM. The phone rang. I did not want other members of my family to wake up. I ran to the lounge and picked up the phone.

No one spoke at first. But then, there were some noises like the wind blowing on the ocean. I kept on saying hello; there was someone who started speaking with ocean sounds in the background—and the person whispered to me, "*the wind is blowing from the north.*" It was a ghostly sound—like that made by ocean tides. I rushed to the phone, so I did not have time to turn on the lights. So, I sat in the dark, listening to the ghostly sound. It was scary. The phone receiver was on my ear but my eyes were looking around in the darkness. I heard it clearly and again, I said hello. But the person kept on saying only one phrase—that *the wind was blowing from the north.* I thought someone was on a ship and was trying to give me some message. I kept on asking myself who it was the whole night.

He kept on repeating the same phrase again and again. I could not understand what the message was. In the dark, I was sitting and the ghostly sound frightened me. I hung up the phone and rushed quickly to my bed. I could not sleep for a while. I kept trying to think what that phone call was about!

The next morning, at my office, one of my company's directors came and asked me about the phone call in strange code. I remembered the phone message. Mr. Rosenthal was sleeping in my guesthouse and he had picked up the phone on a parallel line and heard the message.

I remembered and asked him what that message was. He said that it looked like someone was giving me some message in code! I was wondering what it was! Soon after that, I think the Lord was on his move. Things started moving in a negative direction.

I got sick—was almost on my deathbed. I was having problems in my business but at that time, the director of the company in Zimbabwe came along to my office and said that the Registrar of Companies had made a big mistake and that they had made me the 100% shareholder of the company. I asked him what the problem was. I told him we should go to the company's secretary's office and amend that right then. He thought that I would have played a trick and taken over the entire company. He said that since I was the 100% shareholder, only I had the power to change it. So, he asked me to go and change it. I said that I would, immediately. The procedures took some time. When the documents were ready, I asked him to come the following week so we could go and finalize it with the Secretary. He was very much satisfied. I changed the documentation with the secretary and took the director, Mr. Ronny Zlattner, to the office.

The secretary gave me documents to sign first and then pass over to Ronny, to sign. I signed without even looking at it. So, he asked me why I didn't even read them before signing. I said that I knew what I was doing. After completing all the signing work, I shook hands with him and congratulated him, as he was now the 100% shareholder. He was surprised!

I told him that I was sick and that I'd have to resign from my duties soon. I told him I would not be leaving him immediately, but informed him to find someone to take over from me because I was moving to the USA. It was the time when my daughter Angelina had graduated from Pharmacy College and got married in New York.

It was the wonderful work of God. He did all that in His time and at the right time. I withdrew my personal guarantees to the company and started winding up my affairs in Botswana.

At that time, I realized that Ronny came from the north side of Botswana. The wind blew in my direction. This was the Lord's plan for me.

God did supernatural things to move me from one place to another. I write this again and again because the Lord was with me. The Lord is my shepherd and I shall not want. The Lord helped me all the way till I finally left Botswana.

My Wife Priscilla (Pramila)

Our marriage was matched in heaven, as I explained earlier.

The Bible says: A wife of noble character who can find?

Her husband had full confidence in her.

She brings him good, not harm, all the days of her life.

She gets up while it is still dark; she provides food for her family, and portions for her servant girl.

She watches over the affairs of her household and does not eat the bread of idleness.

Woman who fears the Lord is to be praised.

A good woman is hard to find and worth far more than Diamond.

My marriage was done by His grace. I did not have to find her; the Lord found her for me. In the Holy Bible, in the book of Proverbs, whatever King Solomon wrote exactly fit my wife. The Lord gave me this precious gift.

She was a trained nurse and became WHO (World Health Organization) certified. She was also a Health Visitor and worked in Mandal village, in Viramgaam district of Saurastra, India as the in-charge of the Mandal Health Centre. She helped women by explaining and educating them about birth control and keeping good health. Many women asked her how she knew about pregnancy even though she was such a small, unmarried girl. The villagers were uneducated, backward and superstitious. She had to lie that she was married. They asked where her husband was. She lied further that her husband was in Africa. That lie became true. I went from Africa and got married to her. When I went to the village after our marriage, the ladies were convinced. I believed everything was pre-planned by the Lord. What a blessing was showered on me that my wife is from an originally-Christian family. The Christian history book, *Maru Runne* and a couple of other books written by (whom I called the "walking history") Rev. Menasha, and other Christian history books write highly about the family. I checked online on the computer about Gangaram Dayalji and John Gangaram and found the following history given by the missionaries.

Apostle: Gangaram Dayalji (1843)

I did not know about my wife's family but an old priest, Rev. Manasha Bhuraji, the walking history of Indian Christians, gave me a book named *Maru Runn*. I found the history very interesting. Rev. Manasha wrote history, too, and he wrote about my wife's family. We did not have my wife's grandpa's photo, but we found it in the book.

My wife's father and mother were teachers. Her great, great-grandfather, Gangaram Dayalji, was from the Hindu Lawana caste, of a businessman family. They had a tobacco farming business. He read a Christian pamphlet (tract), which was handed over to him by the Christian Missionary Society. Then, he got hold of the New Testament and read it with full understanding. Thereafter, without anyone's guidance, he believed in Jesus Christ.

If he had not got that tract, he would have been a great Hindu religious head. But he was not satisfied with what he was going through. He read the tract and the New Testament and started proclaiming Jesus Christ as his savior. He met his customers in villages and proclaimed to them that Jesus Christ is God. Rev. William Flower baptized him in Surat.

In Gujarat, he was the first Christian convert and he was the first local teacher in a mission school. In a short time, he went to Vadodara from Surat, with Rev. William Clarkson. Rev. Clarkson wrote about him, saying that if he were to draw Gangaram Dayalji's picture, his eyes would be sparkling. His self-spiritual laughing, proclamation of the gospel as the one true message and explanations with parable examples from his experiences were remarkable. Apostle Gangaram Dayalji Thakker married a girl named Pithila (Pithiba) in 1848. They were married in the Mumbai Free Church mission. Rev. Clarkson loved him so much that he himself got them married.

They had three sons and a daughter. They were very clever and bold. Apostle Gangaram was a strong pillar of the original Church; his oldest son, John, became the first pastor of Surat and the third pastor in the whole of

Gujarat. All three sons were pioneer students at the Boys Christian Training College, which was newly organized in Ahmadabad.

His son, Jacob, was a teacher and spiritual leader. In 1879, his son William was the first headmaster of Anand training school.

Jesus said that if anyone did not give up worldly things, they could not become his disciple. Disciple Gangaram took it very seriously and following the words of Jesus, he surrendered his business, mother, sisters, home and village. He took his cross and walked behind Christ. At the end of his life, to get his reward, he rested in the Lord in a place called Borsad. The Parish felt that their biggest spiritual backing was lost and people mourned him. After his death, his three sons were admitted in a Christian orphanage. He was a steward and he achieved Apostleship as good Christian leader.

Rev. John Gangaram (1893)

John Gangaram was the oldest son of Gangaram Dayalji. He found a job in Ghogha as a teacher. He completed his course as Priest and Evangelist. He was given his license as a priest. He was installed an Evangelist in Surat so that people come to know of him and like him. He was ordained as a pastor of the Surat Church.

He took much interest in the Gujarat and Kathiawar missions and when the Board of Elders was established, he was selected as the first Indian moderator. He was the first leader of the Gujarat mission. In 1918, he suffered a disease called influenza and died in Ahmadabad. He served 46 years in various mission works.

Chhotalal John Thakker

Chhotalal Thakker was the son of John Gangaram. He was an Evangelist sent to Kutch Bhuj, where he became a Pastor but died at the age of 34 years. His wife, Vidyagauri Manohar Desai, became a widow at a very early age. They had four sons and two daughters. Chhotalal was transferred to Ghogha as a Priest. Vidyagauri worked as a teacher. After her husband died in Ghogha, she was transferred to their Rajkot school.

At that time, she saw that wages were very low for missionary workers. So, she came to Ahmadabad. She worked as a teacher in a school in the Calico mill area in Ahmadabad. But unfortunately, teachers were laid off there. So, she was out of job. She found an advertisement in a newspaper that a teacher was required in Karachi. She applied for the job, which she successfully got. She became the Headteacher at that Karachi school.

Vidyagauri was the daughter of a very strong Hindu family of the Desai tribe. Her father was Manohar Desai, known as Ajubhai Bapuji ni Khadki, (Amin) of Naar Gaam, Petlad, Gujarat, India. They were a rich family, known as "Sadawrate" (food distributed to the poor and yet never had any shortage) at their house. Two of the family members are well-known movie actors—Manahar (Malcolm) Desai and Mahesh Desai.

Upkarbhai Ajubhai Desai

My wife's grandmother was Vidyagauri Manoha Desai. Her family Mr. Manoha and Upkarbhai were sons of Ajubhai. Ajubhai worked with Rev R Gillespie, who built the famous Christian village Ranipur (Shahawadi) Church in 1877.

Upkarbhai was a student in Ahmadabad Mission High School. He graduated in 1881 with a Bachelor of Arts (BA) degree. He found a job as an assistant teacher at the same school. After several years, he joined the Bible renewal committee. Dr. Sheledi wrote in his notes that Upkarbhai's help in renewing the Bible into a more modern version of the language was remarkable. Upkarbhai was given the Book of Job, which he renewed in modern rhymes. It became very attractive and we owe him much praise.

Thakker Family

John Gangaram Thakker had good standing as he was ordained Priest at the Surat Church (1893). His son, Chhotalal—my wife's grandfather—died at a very young age. After that, the grandmother, Vidyagauri, had a hard time taking care of the family. She worked as a teacher and finally found a job in Karachi (was in India; is now in Pakistan) as the Principal of a school. She raised her children and lived in Karachi very happily. In 1947, when India and Pakistan was separated, they returned to India and started a new life in Ahmadabad.

My father-in-law, Hamilton Chhotalal Thakker, married a girl from the Panth (well-known poet and writer in the Christian community) family. The family was in Karachi (in India now).

Hamilton Chhotalal Thakker

Mr. Kersondas Panth died at an early age. So, his brother, Mr. Ramji Khimji Panth, raised his children. Among the children was my mother-in-law, Katherine. Ramji Khimji Panth is still well known in the Indian Christian community because he wrote more than 250 Christian songs and translated an important book called *Fabiola*. Both, the father's side and mother's side families were well known in the community of Christians in Gujarat.

I am honored to be the son-in-law of such a noble family. An old priest, Rev. Menasha Bhuraji wrote in his Christian history book about them, with the ancestor's photos, praising them highly. I met Rev. Menasha and spoke about this history of the grandfathers when he gave us the history in length. He gave us the *Panth* songbook, too. The Lord moved me from one house to another, and found a girl for me—just because I prayed and asked him to go before me.

My wife's parents died. Her father died a year after our marriage, and her mother died while alone in Ahmadabad, much later.

The Death of My Mother
(My Travel for the Funeral)

My mother spoke her last words: "Don't touch me. Now, I am holy".

When your mother dies, you lose the biggest part of your life. My mother was a pious lady. When there was no housework, she was always seen with the Bible in her hand, praying. She prayed before eating anything or before putting anything in her mouth. I do the same now. She observed fasts on all Fridays; even when she was sick, she fasted. She fasted through the lent period of 40 days. She used to fast from morning to evening and after our evening prayers, she used to break her fast.

She taught us that when leaving home, we must pray and tell the eldest person of the house that you will be coming soon; not that you are going. All that was our daily practice and all family members followed the same.

On that day, my dad called me from our Bombay home, while I was in Botswana. He could not speak much, so Nelson took over and spoke to me and gave me the sad news that mother had died suddenly.

My Mother's Death And My Testimony

Six months before her death, I was supposed to travel for my Christmas vacation. I booked the beachfront 'Malibu Hotel' in Durban, and paid in advance for the first day.

Everything was set very nicely. We were all excited to go for the vacation. On the Saturday before the planned travel—which was on Sunday morning—I went with my wife and two daughters to my office to arrange all the files and keys in order so that my director from Zimbabwe could deal with bank deposits and checking mail.

I set up everything and returned back home. On the way to my home, which was my daily routine, I passed by a four-way crossroad. I was supposed to go straight and traffic on my right was supposed to stop at the stop sign. A Volkswagen car came rushing toward the stop sign but did not stop. The car came dashing right on my right side. In Botswana and South Africa, cars are right-hand driven. I saw that he was not going to stop so I swung my car to avoid the impact. I did a good job but the car damaged the front fender.

The man went off the road and stopped in a ditch. The city's people knew me and came rushing to see me. We were saved; we did not have any scratches but the car was slightly damaged. The other car's driver was declared dead. The police came and saw that it was his fault. The man in the car was not really dead but he was dead-drunk.

The police knew me and told me to come to the police station the next day. I went to the police station the next day. The man who was drunk was locked up. After showing my driving license and car registration, the police, though I was not at fault, told me not to file any charges on the other man. I was furious but the police officer explained that he was an army soldier and he the son of the biggest chief of the biggest tribe of Northern Botswana. The police said that it would not help but only harm me if I did press charges.

Anyway, I could not travel the next day. So, I was thinking about why that happened to me. I called my dad in India and spoke to him. He asked me when I was coming. I said that I wasn't going that year. He said that my mother was waiting for me.

At that time, I changed my mind and cancelled my Durban tour. I immediately bought tickets to India. We started our journey. We were supposed to get on a flight from Johannesburg. So, I drove 700 miles to Johannesburg in the same car—which was fixed on Sunday morning and I started my journey the same evening. I left my car with a businessman and asked him to get it fixed. We took a direct flight to Mumbai. The next morning, we reached home. My mum was in bed and my dad was thrilled seeing us all arrive. He had a good time with our two daughters.

They looked very happy. I was by my mother's bedside for four days. Though she was sick, she cooked good food for us and even when she was not sick anymore, she looked tired.

We went to visit our sisters and other family members all over India. We had a good time and finally, we returned.

At the airport, I usually did not look back, but this time, I looked back and my mum and dad were looking at us. I went back and hugged my mother and dad. With tears and a heavy heart, we returned.

After six months, I received the call that mum was with the Lord. We were grieving but I praised the Lord for he made me meet with the accident so that I could see my mother. God works in mysterious ways. We often question the Lord asking him why he did this or that. But I have seen how the Lord works for us.

Our Life in Botswana

We lived in a commercial town called Francistown, which was located in the famous Kalahari Desert. It was a one-street town. There was no clean water or adequate medical facilities. Deserts are usually very hot during the daytime and very cold during the nights. Kalahari has it's natural beauty; the sun, the sand and salt pans, the charming Okavango Delta, exciting Chobe National park, Moremi game reserve, Makgadikgadi Pan National Park, Nxai Pan and many more wildlife game reserves and fabulous evenings with colorful skies and wonderful sunsets. We were in the middle of all that beauty and the beasts. The small place had its problems, too. The lack of medical facilities was our biggest problem. The local people were very good; very helpful and sympathetic. Most of the local people usually went to witchdoctors for medical treatments.

We had a nice house with a housemaid working very nicely; she was just like our family member. The garden boy worked in our garden.

There were two incidents at our house. Our maid used to get a bucket of water from outside to wipe the floor daily because it became muddy. One day, she brought the bucket into our bedroom to wipe the floor. Under the bucket, there was an African Black Scorpion. She was sweeping the floor and found the black scorpion in our bedroom. She thought it was one of the children's toys. So, she reached for the scorpion using her hand and she saw the scorpion move. She was stunned and immediately killed the scorpion with one smack of our slipper. Black scorpions are very dangerous because they are very poisonous.

One day, our maid and garden boy were sitting outside, on our garden veranda. The boy was from a village in the jungle. He told the maid that there was a snake around. She asked where. He said that he could smell the snake. She asked him if he could smell snakes, while laughing at him. The boy started searching for the snake. The maid did not believe him.

There were some cardboard boxes nearby; he started searching them for the snake and he found a snake coiled up and fast asleep. The maid called my wife over the phone. I was away for a meeting in the Zimbabwe office. My wife was sitting in my office. She rushed with our main supervisor of the factory.

The man saw the snake and said that it was a Spitting Cobra. He took one shot at the snake and the snake woke up and stood straight in front of the man. He took another aim and the snake was dead. We lived with the most poisonous animals around our house.

I was very busy taking care of my factories and my wife was running our retail shops. We both worked hard and were taking care of our children. We were always thinking of the best education and best lives for our children because we ourselves did not have such opportunities. We were alone; we had no family around us, taking care of us. We were the only Indian Christian family in the country.

My Brother Augustine

Augustine was our delicate brother. When he was less than one year old, he was sick. The baby had infection that spread into his rib bones. Those days there was no cure for bacterial infections. For infections, there were no medications. People used to die out of simple pneumonia.

Augustine was in hospital with a tube in his left-side rib and the other end of the tube in a bottle, dripping with pus. The doctors were cutting one rib after the other and when he used to feel fine, he smiled at us all the time. When he smiled, we were got excited and played with him.

He had nine surgeries as an infant. After the eighth surgery, the doctors said he was well and we could take him home. We brought him home with a big bandage on his chest. We were all happily getting ready on Easter Sunday to go to church, but him being a little baby, mum got him ready first and placed him on a table to play with us. We were all ready to leave for church and mum picked him up. As soon as she picked him up, the bandage was notably full of pus and stinking. The side was open. We rushed him to hospital. He was taken to the emergency room where they cleaned his side, put a new bandage on and put him back on the bed with the tube dripping pus into bottle. We were sad and did not celebrate the day. We bought balloons and gave them to him to play—to make him happy.

The next day, the doctor came and said we will do his surgery for the last time. It was his ninth surgery. But the very next day, the doctor did not do the surgery. He came to discuss with my dad and mum that a doctor from England had come with a new medication and he will try on your son. It was government free hospital. We had no choice but accept whatever comes.

The doctors did the surgery on Wednesday following the Easter Sunday. Everything was set and the parents were allowed to see the surgery through a glass window. The doctors said that they would try their best. God willing, he will be cured with the new medications.

The medicine was Penicillin. It was newly invented medication. The doctor broke glass injection bottle and sprinkled over the infected area, cutting all the rotten sides out. My mother, at that time, prayed looking what doctors were doing. She prayed and spoke to the Lord; these were the words "Lord if my son comes out from this surgery, I will give the boy for your work. Please save him."

The Lord heard the prayer and Augustine got cured completely. He was kept in hospital for two more weeks. He was given the Penicillin injections. We celebrated his first birthday in Hospital. I remember dad buying a tricycle for him. We brought him home. Our granny (father's mother Laxmi/Lalima) stayed in the hospital—day and night—24/7 with the baby, taking care of him all the time. I must say; she took good care of the baby. Augustine was given life through my Mum's prayer. We are sure that the Lord hears our prayers.

When he was sent to school, the teachers were given special instructions not to touch him. In India, teachers used to punish children by striking them on hands or legs—wherever they felt like. His teacher told him that if I come near you, just shout that you areAugustine.

He graduated from high school and we sent his tickets from Africa to come and work with me. My dad wanted to get him to Africa to help in my business.

He came when I had business with my partner, Mr. Dhirubhai Naik, originally from Astagaam in Navsary, Gujarat. My dad lived with them in their house. He was very kind to us. My dad and Augustine lived in that house. When I left Ndola for starting a business in Lusaka, Augustine was with them working for our business but Dhirubhai changed his mind and we were separated in business. My dad and Augustine were still there with them as paying guests.

Thereafter, I was well-settled in my business in Lusaka. After about six months, I went to Ndola to see my dad and Augustine. I saw Augustine was not comfortable being lonely. I asked Dhirubhai that I am taking my brother with me. He agreed and said; take him away; I don't need him. I asked my brother to pack his bag and took him to Lusaka. We both worked in Lusaka and lived with Divecha family. When he came from India, I already taught him driving car in Ndola. He was already a driver, and shuttled between Lilayi and Lusaka for our business. After about six months, my dad told me that I should go to India and get married. I left Augustine to take care of the shop and went to India for my marriage. Augustine was educated in Mumbai's Premier high school, Dadar.

He had already graduated from his high school. When he came there were airplane services, so he could fly to Africa.

After my wife came to Africa, Augustine was like our son. He used to demand that his choice of food be cooked. Every week, he had his choice of food prepared.

We were now three in my shop so he came with his proposal that he wants to go for further studies. He already had some friends going to the college for the course of Electronic Engineering, a course from England, "City and Guild" certificate. He went with his friends to get admission at the school but the principal did not accept his application because his English was not good.

The very next day, I went to see the principal and spoke to him about his problems. He was a high school graduate which was the requirement, fulfilled, but his spoken English was not good. After convincing the principal, he accepted him with a condition that the teachers would review his case in six months' time. Augustine was allowed sitting on the last bench. Fortunately, his teacher was a South African Indian who took good care of him. Augustine passed his first test and he was allowed to study further in his college.

He graduated from the college in four years' time and achieved the "City of Guild" of London certificate.

After graduating, the department of telecommunication gave him a training job. A company hired him on temporary basis, to install new phones in Intercontinental Hotel, which was newly built Hotel. When my dad came from Ndola one weekend, he took us to show the work he had done. We had tea in the garden together and saw the hotel and the rooms where he installed the phones.

Augustine found that there was opportunity to go to America for further education in electronics. He applied to the college and he was admitted. He went to California and there, he made his way to getting a green card and ultimately his citizenship.

Augustine was well set and he had his own a business 7/11 shop. He went to get married and married my wife's younger sister, Manorama (Edna) and lived in Van Nuys, Los Angeles, California. They have three children—Amit, Ashish and Amisha.

The Death of Augustine

Augustine spoke to me over the phone about six months before his death. He said that he believed that it was his time to go, as he was not feeling well. Augustine seemed unhappy with his health because he was feeling sick. Maybe the Lord had spoken to him and hence, he came out with those words. I told him not to say that as he was too young to even think about that. In December, he had chest pain. He was popping Nitroglycerin every fifteen minutes, at night. He did not inform anyone but kept quiet about it. That night, he went to the toilet and collapsed there. He shouted to get his wife to come. His wife saw him in a bad condition and called 911 for help. The ambulance arrived and he was taken to hospital but it was too late. The Emergency Ward tried all treatments but he did not respond. Augustine left us with lots of memories.

My Sisters

I mentioned to my dad once that one teardrop of any of my sisters' is worth my entire capital. I loved my sisters because they were the dearest to me; I used to visualize them in my dreams. When we met, we celebrated and loved each other's company. My older sister, Freny loved us and was good help to our mother and us.

My sister Violet was with me always, during our school time. We used to study together, sharing one table and a table lamp for our exams. I used to write letters to my mum after arriving in Ndola. When Violet wrote to me, she asked why I had written in a rural language. I then realized that my language had changed because I lived with villagers. Violet sent me a gift—a round, old-time record. It had a *qawali* song (Islamic-type song) from a popular Indian movie. I played it several times and used to visualize my sister, with tears in my eyes.

My sister Lina was in her primary school when I left for Africa. She was in high school when I returned, the first time, from Africa. She was a grown-up young girl with lots of talents including singing. When I visited her after she got married and was living in the Borivli area of Mumbai, she gave me a gift. It was a pair of cufflinks, which I had treasured for a long time. I treasured all my memories and am now sharing it all in this testimony. My sister Rosemary loved me so much that she accompanied me when I went to select a girl for my marriage. When I visited my Valsad house, she visited me frequently. At one time, she brought Khaja, Ghari (Indian sweets) and a basket full of mangoes only for me to eat because those particular kinds of mangos were not available in Africa.

My sister, Irene—I remember her from when she was in a convent primary school. I used to hold her hand and cross the road because the school was in front of our house across the road. One day, when I went to pick her up, she was in tears. I asked her what happened but she could not answer; she only wept—loudly. I took her home crying. But at home, she told us that in class, they were singing a song called "Irene, goodnight" and she didn't like that they sang a song with her name in it. We all laughed and felt sorry for her naive behavior. When I returned after 11 years in Africa, she was a teenager. After that, she was in college. Time flies—she got married and I attended her wedding. The only wedding I attended in all my brother and sister's wedding celebrations was Irene's.

My baby sister Bimba (Mabel) was only about three years old when I left India. I remember that every morning, she used to come by dad and begin complaining about some pain she had, itching here and there, thinking that we will feel sorry for her. She was like a doll in our house. I do not know when she grew up and was married. I remember visiting her after her marriage, at Gandhinagar, a city near Ahmadabad. I visited her on one trip when she had just had her first child—her son Carroll. When I entered the house, I saw that the boy looked yellow and immediately said that he had jaundice. She was surprised to note that I could see the symptoms of disease. I gave the boy the name 'Pitamber' (a Hindu god with yellow clothing). I still call him that when I am with my sister.

My Brothers

I remember that my older brother, Nelson, was often chastised by my mother, as is often the case with oldest children. Being the eldest, lots of work was given to him and he did lots of unique things as well. He was the best singer in our neighborhood. Once, there was a competition of talents in our building. About three boys of his age sang but my brother sang the best. But the judge was biased and said that the award must be given to the other boy because my brother sang two songs and the competition was for only one song. When I left India, Nelson was already working as a clerk in an office. He worked in an orphanage near Nasik (Maharashtra state) city. When I returned from Africa, I visited him and stayed one night at his house. He lived in the Chembur area of Mumbai. It was nice to be with the brother and my sister-in-law. That was the only time I stayed with them in India. When he settled in Africa, he took us to an International hotel, where previously Augustine has installed telephones, and there we had buffet lunch. I could see that he was very happy seeing that I was enjoying lunch with him. In his California house, he always goes above and beyond entertaining us with meals.

Augustine's history is written in length in this testimony. He was the youngest, most fragile and loving brother of all. He filed petitions for all our brother and sisters. He got us all settled in America. His wife Manorama entertained all of us when we first entered America. Augustine had to bear lots of difficulties settling the families but he did all that smilingly. He was born to settle the family in America. Maybe, that was the purpose of our Lord. He is with the Lord now but cannot be forgotten for his work and hospitality towards to all our families.

Uncle Wilson

Our youngest uncle Wilson did his Masters in English Language and found a job in Ahmadabad, Gujarat. His history is unique. He grew up with us in Mumbai. He studied at the Wilson College, Mumbai. He was in the same class as the Maharaja of Vansda, of Dang district. The Maharaja once told me that he used to have running competitions with Wilson Hatia. He was always number one in running competitions. So, the Maharaja used to tease him saying 'Hatia, Hatia, *Marghi na tatia.*' (Hatia, Hatia, chicken legs.) I laughed and agreed with him that my uncle was always first in races. I'd seen him running for the church and winning a medal.

He was dark in complexion but he looked very handsome. He had lots of hair and had a celebrity-like hairstyle. One evening, he came home with a black cap—like what my grandfather used to wear. After shaving his hair, he was ashamed to show himself to us so he wore a typical Indian hat in black color. We were shocked to see that he was completely bald. My mother was furious and asked him why he did that. Usually, a young man like him, in Hindu religious rituals, shaved their hair when his mother or father died. But he'd shaved it just for fun.

When he started with his first job, he brought sweets for us from his first salary. He brought us some fresh cream pastry called Malai Na khaja. We really appreciated it very much.

Wilson uncle was a good singer, too. He used to have a bath every morning and then he used to comb his hair, singing all the songs of Tansen's (A famous singer from India). After getting ready, he used to have his breakfast and go to college.

He was educated in English. He did not know to read or write Hindi or Gujarati. His command over the English language was excellent. He did well in his teaching job.

I remember the application he wrote for his first job; it said, 'I learn more by teaching.'

One day, our pastor's wife came with a girl to our house and requested my uncle Wilson to coach her in the English language, for her examination. He agreed to go and teach the girl at the pastor's home itself. There, he fell in love with her and decided to marry her. She came to our family as a surprise. This marriage was matched in heaven. We did not know her family but the pastor's wife persuaded and convinced my mother to get them married.

His spoken Gujarati improved very much in Ahmadabad. My parents wanted him to settle down well.

He was married after I got married. I could not attend his wedding because I was in Africa. He could not find a girl for himself even though there were many girls who tried to be friends with him.

He is with the Lord; he died a peaceful, natural death. His family members are my aunty Bakul-*kaki*, a daughter named Audrey/Rupal and a son named Bertrand/ Bertie. We lived very far from each other but we loved each other dearly.

While my dad and I were in Africa, we tried to get Uncle Wilson to Lusaka, Zambia. We had a good friend from our church, a manager of schools in Lusaka. We went to his home after the church service. My dad spoke to him about Wilson uncle, his education and his teaching experience at the college. The manager offered him a job at a high school in Lusaka. My dad wrote to my uncle about a good job with a salary that was 10 times more than what he got at the college in Ahmadabad—plus a chance to be a principal at the school. My uncle wrote back saying he was a professor in a college and would not like to be degraded just for money. I didn't know whether it was his ego, profession or position, but I admired his self-confidence.

Emanuel Uncle (Emu-Kaka)

Emanuel, or 'Emu-*kaka*' as we used to call him, used to study under kerosene lamps at night for his high school state final exam. He knew that his mother couldn't afford his studies so he worked hard. His father was in Iraq. He was the most brilliant student in the whole school. He went to give his higher secondary school's all-India test. He was expected to be among the top ten students in the test but when the result came out, he was declared to have failed.

The principal of the school could not believe it. He paid a fee of ten rupees for rechecking his papers. Once this was done, the answer came that all the evening papers were written one line over the other. They then found out that he was going blind. It was already too late to cure his ophthalmic condition. Medical facilities were not like these days. My uncle lost his eyesight and became completely blind.

He became helpless, but he did not lose his hope in Jesus Christ. He was a brilliant student but he knew he would not be able to study any further. He was trying to get a job, but who would give a blind man a job?

He was in Bombay—the busiest and one of the most congested cities of India. He wanted to be a self-reliant individual. He applied for a job in a blind school in Tardev, an area in Bombay. He was hired immediately. His English knowledge and his scholastic knowledge were very good. He became a teacher in a blind school.

He found a house near the school. The house was about four miles from the school, so he had to take a bus to go home. Three stops from the school and he'd reach home. From the bus stop, his house was nearby but he had to cross the busy road. Fortunately, there was a kiosk near the bus stop. The kiosk owner used to come to his help and used to walk with him, crossing the road. He then reached his house with the help of a cane. It was very hard to live like that but he wanted to do everything on his own. He used to visit us every weekend and had lunch and dinner with us.

Suddenly, we did not see him for three months. My dad and I went looking for him. We found him in a shanty home. He was married to a lady from Ramabai mission, near Bombay. Her name was Shushila. My dad saw that his wife was completely blind, too.

My dad was furious and told him that a blind cannot lead another blind. But he argued that he wanted to help a helpless lady who could understand what he was going through. It was not a clever decision but he was happy with his wife and Shushila aunty was also very smiley and happy. When he used to visit us at our home, he used to teach us how to play the harmonium (keyboard-like instrument). He used to play it and sing along, too. One of his songs, I still remember, was one that went: *"Harsh Watito maala lay harsh watito." (Marathi language)*

("I am overwhelmed, I am very much overwhelmed")

My uncle used to massage patients at hospitals; he was a good masseur.

He was good with his hands. He used to knit chair seats with cane strips. He made patterns by just touching them with his figures. He was a really talented person.

One day, we got a message that they had a baby boy. My dad and I went to see how they managed to nurse the baby. They named the baby Steven. Steven was crawling on the sandy ground. I saw that they had tied a few bells—like cowbells—around the baby's waist so that when he moved, they could find him. It was my uncle's brilliant idea. I went to meet uncle and the aunty and spoke to both of them about any help they might need from us. The uncle gave me a stool to sit on and I could see that aunty was cooking on a stove, with a smile on her face. That was my last visit to their home.

A few years later, they had a second son. After his birth, my aunty lost her mind. She started speaking in weird languages and acted like she'd lost her mind. My uncle took her to a nearby hospital but from there, she was taken and admitted in a psychiatric hospital in a suburb called Thana. Uncle Emanuel, my mum and I went to visit her to see what was happing.

She was speaking like she was out of her mind. It was not nice to see that she was given electric shocks on her head. Her hair was falling out or being burned out. We could not see her clearly because the authorities would not allow us to see her personally. We saw her through the iron bars. She spoke to us in mixed messages.

About two weeks later, she died at the hospital. Uncle Emanuel and Uncle Simon met us at the Thana Psychiatric Hospital. My mum and I went to the hospital with a sheet of knitted fresh flowers. We call it a knitted sheet (*chaddar*) of flowers. We bought a few garlands for the funeral. The body was handed over to us. There were no funeral services in the city. We had to do all the procedures on our own. We brought a hand-driven cart, covered it with a round canopy, which we covered with a white sheet and on the top of the white sheet, we put the flower-knitted sheet and flower garlands. My uncle Emanuel bought some garlands locally. We were five of us taking the funeral cart to the church, which was arranged a day before. Emu-*kaka*, Chhotu-*kaka* (Simon), Alfred-*mama* (mother's maternal uncle), my mother and I. Behind the church was a cemetery. The priest performed the funeral prayers and we buried Shushila-*kaki* in Thana. We saw a snake passing by at the time of the ceremony, but it was a little far from us.

Now, the problem was who was going to take care of the two children. We took both the sons to granny. It was not possible for my mother to take care of the two children because we were already nine of us in one small apartment. The decision was taken that the children would remain under the care of our grandmother Lalima. My granny lived with Uncle Simon, who was also blind. My aunty, Lily-*kaki*, had one son and one daughter then. So, we took the little newborn baby there with the older son, Steven. The day we took those two kids, Steven was well adjusted with their son Pravin (Hector), but the newborn son, named Augustine, (nicknamed Gorbhai) was too small. We kept him on a bed all the time, wrapped up in a sheet. I still visualize little Gorbhai sleeping on the bed. Simon uncle gave him the name Gorbhai. He said that he was sweet—like a lump of jaggery (brown palm sugar). Gorbhai is now over 60 years of age but he is still called Gorbhai. The funny part of it is that many of our family members do not know his real name.

Steven grew up with the family. My uncle Simon used to call him every morning to read the newspaper for him. He read the newspaper every day for uncle. The practice of reading the newspaper helped Steven with general knowledge and he became a brilliant student in school. The only thing I know of him is that he graduated with a Bachelor's in Engineering and started working at Crompton Greaves, a company known to be ceiling-fan manufacturers. Now, Steven is in the USA with his wife Beulah; they have two children.

Gorbhai married and had one son. He worked as a teacher and lived a very poor life—but he was very happy with his family. When I visited India, I met him at our church in Bombay. He was a short man whom I could not recognize. He introduced himself and I was shocked to see him after a long time. I saw him when he was just born. I saw him at the church and when I came to know that he was Augustine (Gorbhai), I simply threw myself at him and hugged him. He asked me to come to his house. My wife and I decided to go with him because it was Christmas time and he was celebrating the festival with his family. Nobody from our family visited him like he'd mentioned, so we went with him. I hired a taxi and went with him. On the way, he asked me to stop at Borivli Station. The taxi stopped and he went to buy a Christmas cake. The shop was called Mongia Cakes. He had booked this cake a week in advance. He came with the cake and said that that was the best cake in the world. I smiled looking at my wife. The poor boy had not seen the world but this cake was the best in his world. He was so happy that we were visiting him. I saw his house; it was a small hut but a very comfortable one. He had his wife and his parents-in-law with him. I respected them and greeted them. We had cake together and some soft drink. Thereafter, I met him at a family wedding in Baroda. He was sickly but he sat by me and did not speak much. That was the last I saw of him.

Unfortunately, Gorbhai had diabetes, which was not in control and he was often hospitalized. He died at a very young age. I still keep in touch with his wife and son.

Simon Uncle

My uncle Simon was a 'happy-go-lucky' person. He used to crack jokes all the time. He became blind at a very young age. He was working at the water pipeline station, keeping records of the flow of the water. He used to give reports of water flow or damages in the pipeline communicating with the head office. He used to get the meter reading on a Richter scale-like device that made graphic-like lines. I use to see that and get fascinated by all the graphic lines and clock-like meters.

He had a phone in his office and I had access to a phone at my high school. My mum used to give me a written message and I used get the help of my class teacher to phone my uncle and give him those messages. The usual message was that he should visit us during weekends for the celebration of one of our birthdays or on a festive weekend.

Simon uncle became blind. He had some sickness like diphtheria with a high fever. Those days, diagnosis was not accurate. There was no technology like in modern days. Those days, doctors gave medications based on naturopathy and allopathy. We had home remedies for cold and cough but those were not always effective. In that age, my uncle lost his both eyes due to the high fever or some other disease which was not known.

He worked at the Tulsi pipeline water pump station and, though he was blind, he could dial phones very accurately and speak to the officers in Hindi, Marathi, and English—which was not common—with promptness. There were no complaints about his disability.

Simon uncle had a good government job. So, a proposal came from a Christian family that there was a girl from an orphanage who had come on a vacation to live with her uncle. The uncle used to work for the railways so he lived in the railway quarters at Santacruz station. Near the family lived, our distantly-related maternal uncle, named Alexander. He brought the marriage proposal for Simon uncle.

My mum took me with her to see the girl who was prepared to marry a blind man. We saw that there were two sisters, Lily and Shanti, coming from an orphanage near Valsad. They had a brother named Samuel, who worked as a fireman in a small railway station named Udhna near Surat.

When Samuel got married, Simon uncle, Lily aunty, Walter-*mama* and I were present in Udhna. We were there a week in advance for the wedding arrangements. Udhna was a small railway station. It was like a patch of beauty in the wilderness. The wedding party started from Udhna by train and reached Valsad in the evening. We had a good celebration in Valsad.

Their parents had died when they were toddlers. They were sent to the orphanage where they grew up. They were two helpless sisters living in poverty with the good uncle, but his wife was behaving very badly with those girls.

My mother called the oldest girl, Lily, to come and talk to us. She walked to us silently and stood by us. My mother patted her and asked her whether she was prepared to marry a blind man. She agreed immediately to avoid the abuse of the aunty. In my opinion, all this was the plan of our Lord.

The marriage was arranged in a nearby Marathi church in the Andheri suburb of Bombay, near the Santa Cruz Airport. We went walking to the church and the immediate family members attended the marriage. Thereafter, we took a train to our home in Dadar.

We reached home with the newly-wedded couple uncle Simon and Aunty Lily. We used to call her Lily-*kaki*. (*Kaki* means uncle's wife) Among all our brothers and sisters, she loved me the most. I liked her, too.

On the very first day, my mother asked her to prepare some tea for all of us. She was preparing tea on a primus stove. The tea with milk was almost overflowing due to the flame. She looked for a utensil to hold the hot pot. I was standing by her. She found a pair of pliers and picked up the pot using them. In India, the brass pots did not have handles. She found a carpenter's pliers and picked up the overflowing hot pot.

I was only ten years old so I announced to everyone that aunty used a carpenter's tool to pick up the teapot.

My mother came rushing to the kitchen and we all laughed about the act in the kitchen by the newly-married aunty. Lily aunty was always seen smiling. She always looked shy and smiled in shyness.

My grandmother used to live with my uncle Simon because there was no one to care for the blind uncle. After marriage, he had a good life, getting good food cooked at home. Uncle Simon had four children—three boys and a girl.

I used to go to the uncle's home during my school vacations. He worked in water works department and also had family run a small kiosk selling cigarettes, biscuits, hair oils, sodas and allied items like daily requirements. I used to love sitting with my uncle in the shop. He needed my help because I became his eyes. I used to look after the shop well.

One day, a man named Barkusukha, who was working in the same department as Simon uncle, was sacked for being disabled in one eye. He was a laborer in the same department, who laid pipes. He was blind in his left eye. When his superiors sacked him, he argued with the department and lodged a complaint through the labor union that he was blind in one eye but Simon was blind in both eyes but was still working.

The department asked my uncle to go to the government hospital and get reports of his eyes. This incident, I clearly remember, A Parsi (a family of ex-Iranian-immigrant origin) doctor who spoke Gujarati checked my uncle's eyes and said that he was sorry about his job. He mentioned that even if Simon had slight vision in his eyes, he would have given him a certificate of fitness, but he was completely blind.

There was no argument because we knew that that was the fact. The department gave my uncle a one-month notice period and he lost his job. Barkusukha came to know about my uncle losing his job because of him. He came to him and apologized for the mistake. But nothing could bring back the job—not only the job, he had to leave the government housing too and moved into a small rented house.

Fortunately, one of the officers in the department sympathized with my uncle because my uncle had clean records in the department and was an educated man. The officer offered a job to my aunty, Simon's wife, as a nurse-helper in a municipal hospital near the house. She joined and became a fully-qualified nurse in one year. Aunty became a nurse and she was given a permanent job with a municipal house in the water works department. My uncle lived in poverty but the Lord blessed him with three sons and a daughter. Two of the sons I managed to emigrate to Africa and they are well settled. The eldest son and the sister stayed back in India. Simon uncle's children are married and they are in good positions.

Divine Power

Another amazing blessing

I wrote several times that God works in mysterious ways. I witnessed this once more.

There was an accident at my house. My housemaid was in the kitchen and I was at the dining table with my wife, mum and dad. The girl was trying to open a hot pressure cooker. I was done eating my lunch, so I went to the kitchen and saw that Alice was trying to open the hot pressure cooker. I bent down to stop her but by then she used all her might and opened the cooker. The hot water splashed on my chest and belly. It could have been worse but I had clothing on me. I was badly burnt. I had first aid given by the local physician who covered the wound with a bandage.

The next day, the bandage was stinking and I had fever. I realized that the bandage was not a good idea. But I did not remove it. I took a driver with me and drove through to the Mater Dei Hospital Bulawayo, Zimbabwe.

From Francistown to Bulawayo in Zimbabwe, it took about two and a half hours. It's only a 200-mile distance but both countries' borders took a long time to clear people through immigration and customs formalities.

I call Dr. Civin, wife of the Zimbabwe director. She asked me to come to her clinic. But by the time we reached Bulawayo, I had high fever. So, I went straight to the Mater Dai Hospital.

The nurse at the hospital called Dr. Civin to inform that I was already admitted in the hospital. Dr. Civin was furious but she came immediately. She asked me why I did not go to her clinic. I told her that I had high fever and that her clinic was in the middle of the city and the hospital was nearer to me.

Anyway, the nurses were given instructions and by evening, I was feeling much better and I could sleep peacefully. Maybe, I was given sedatives.

I had to stay in hospital for 14 days. I was fine the next day so I went to have a bath with some antiseptic medication in the tub. I did that every day. I did that every morning at 7 AM. Then, I came to my bed and immediately opened my Bible. I sat on my bed and read the Bible and said my prayers.

There were six beds in the ward. I was sleeping in the middle bed but on both sides, the beds were empty. But in front of me, there were three beds with patients. They were Zimbabwe-European patients. They saw me doing everything exactly at 7 AM and reading the Bible after that. After finishing my devotion at about 7.30 AM, the breakfast came. One of the three patients asked me what I was reading every morning. He thought that I was either Hindu or Muslim.

I told him that I read the Bible and I say my prayers. Without my shower and devotion, I do not start my day. All three of them started asking me if I was Christian. I said yes, and asked them about their religion. They said we are Christians, too. I was very happy and asked them to come with me to the Chapel on Saturday because we had church service on Saturday at the hospital's chapel. All three of them agreed to come with me.

The chapel was on the fifth floor. On Saturday, I took all three of them to the chapel. We were in our hospital clothing and gowns.

We entered the church, where the priest and deacon of the local Anglican Church were present. About 10 other believers were present there. We sat down on the pews but two of the three walked out in a few minutes. I ran behind them and asked them to just sit and see what we do. But they did not come in again. One of the three remained seated by me. He was looking down at all times. He stood up or sat down following me. He was quiet and did not even sing hymns but just sat, looking down. I opened the Bible, the hymns book and the book of devotional liturgy and showed him, to follow.

After the church service, we were given Holy Communion but he did not take it.

I asked him, quietly, to take but he did not.

After the communion, we had our last prayer. During the time of the prayer, I heard him crying loudly. I opened my eyes and saw him with lots of tears. I thought that he was having pain because he was patient at the hospital.

The priest and catechist came rushing and asked him what had happened!

We all asked him together and he looked down, crying. With tears, he said that he had not attended church in a long time. He said that he used to go to church when he was a small boy, with his grandpa and grandma.

He said that he had attended church after many years that day—thanks to the Indian man that brought me to the church; it reminded me of my parents and grandparents. After that, the priest and catechist put their hands on him and prayed. He took the Holy Communion and became very happy. We sang our last hymn for him and dispersed.

We returned to the ward and met the other two patients. They said; there is no God. I asked them who created this world and everything in it. He argued that it was just nature. I said if it is just nature, someone must have created the nature. But they did not want to believe in Jesus.

After that, I forgot all about the incident. About two months later, when I attended the Anglican Church synod in Gaborone, Botswana, Rt. Rev. Bishop Khotso Mukhudu came looking for me during the break time. He was with a priest from Bulawayo, Zimbabwe. In a few weeks, he said that he would be in the Francistown Parish as our Parish Priest. I was happy to meet my priest, Father Maruleng.

Father Maruleng asked me what I had done. I asked him what I had done. He told me that a family had given testimony that an Indian man, Mr. Samuel, brought them to church. He had given my name and said that I was from Francistown. So, the Father wanted to meet me—because he was assigned to be the Priest of the Francistown Parish.

After Synod Father Maruleng returned to the Bulawayo Parish, I was the main steward and parish treasurer of the Francistown Parish in Northern Botswana. There were 14 villages—small village congregations—under my care. One month later, Father Maruleng was transferred to my parish and he spoke to the parishioners about the family and my contribution.

The Lord works in mysterious ways. I was hospitalized and put into jeopardy just to save that family. Praise the Lord, for he used me for His work. The family attended church in Bulawayo where Father Maruleng was the priest. Father Maruleng mentioned that the family came in much earlier to the church, and sat on the front bench with their two children.

Heart Problems

I had several health issues because I had work tension. In 1974, I had problems balancing. I felt that something was wrong with me. I went to see a doctor in Bulawayo. Dr. Desai, my good friend, referred me to a neurologist who operated from Salisbury. Fortunately, he was in Bulawayo on that day. He was a very busy doctor, being the 2nd best in the world. The doctor just put his hand at the back of my neck and told me to go to Salisbury (now Harare) for a series of tests. I thought that he was trying to make money out of me. I did not go to Salisbury but returned back to Botswana.

After two days, Dr. Desai called over the phone and asked what I was doing in Botswana since I was supposed to go to Salisbury. I told him that he did not check me at all and that he just placed his finger on my neck and told me to go to his clinic for more tests. Dr. Desai told me that I could have had a stroke and it could be very serious. The left side of my body was cold.

The next day, I flew to Salisbury. The doctor met me in his office and booked a hospital bed for me. I was hospitalized and the following day, the doctor gave me an injection in my neck. It was like a dye for the arteries; he took a series of X-rays. It was extremely painful. The doctor found a blood clot in the right side of my neck and he gave me two kinds of medications—one for anticlotting and the other for blood circulation. It took two years for me to feel warmth in my left side.

Heart problems In the December of 1990, I had heart problems. I had chest pain but I did not worry about it. It so happened that my wife was coming from USA via London to Bulawayo Airport on Sunday.

I called my cardiologist the day before, on a Saturday night. He was at a wedding party but asked me to come at 9 AM on Sunday. My wife was also arriving at the same time. I asked my friend, Parshottam Giga, to go to the airport and I went to see my doctor.

The Lord was always with me. The medical center was closed on Sunday, but the Doctor came and the whole center was opened just for me. The doctor checked my heart condition and told me to go to Johannesburg and see a cardiologist. But the cardiologist was very busy man. So, it was difficult to get an appointment. He said that he could make an appointment for me but it would take three months before I got an appointment. I told the doctor that I would get appointment in one week. I called my business associates in Johannesburg and asked them to get me an appointment. On Wednesday, I flew to Johannesburg. My associate businessman came with me and I had a full check-up on Thursday. The Cardiologist and my business friend were good friends. They arranged for me to go to the hospital instead of staying at the hotel.

I was hospitalized and had an Angiogram the next day. The Angiogram and Angioplasties took a total of 45 minutes but the doctor turned on the light in 15 minutes and said that I had to go for a by-pass surgery.

I was alone; I had no one to share my agony with. I wept on that day but four nurses came to me and comforted me. The doctor came and said that I needn't worry as these kinds of surgeries were done every day. I called my friend and my wife in Botswana. She was very busy in her shop because it was Christmas-business month.

My wife had to close her shop and come travelling 1000 kms with one of my friends. She arrived at 7 PM to see me at the hospital and broke down in tears. We had no time on that day because it was our bedtime.

She'd travelled such a long distance so my friend and his family took her home. My Johannesburg office's main director, Mr. Al Hyman, came with his wife, Doctor Civin, who treated my burn pain at the Meter-Dei hospital in Bulawayo. They now lived in Johannesburg.

He was very concerned about my surgery. He helped me in getting a power of attorney to transfer power to my wife. Mr. Al Hyman's daughter was a partner in the biggest lawyer's firm of Africa. She went to the office and prepared the power of attorney documents for me. She took my signature and went to get the signature of a magistrate at his home. She then brought the papers to me and handed them over to my wife. She did all that work for free. It was a precaution taken so that, just in case, I did not make it through the surgery, my wife could act on my behalf in my affairs.

On Sunday morning, Dr. Civin took permission from the hospital, and I was driven to the director's office and told to sit on his chair and call all my relatives and speak to them for any length of time. Those days, phone calls to America were very costly. I called my children and spoke to them for a long time. It was the day my wife and I had a busy time. In the evening, we sat in a quiet corner of the garden at the Mil-Park hospital. With tears, we looked at each other like I was going to the gallows the next morning.

Second Heart attack

Heart surgery was new those days. During my surgery, the brother of Dr. Bernard, founder of the heart surgery, was on the team. My surgery was done successfully and I recovered fully. I was back to normal life but in seven months' time, I had chest pain again. This time, it was more severe than the previous one.

Fortunately, I was on the highway entering Johannesburg. I was with my driver. We drove straight to the Mil-Park hospital. Dr. Cassel, my consulting cardiologist, checked me and immediately, I was taken to the operation theater for an angiogram.

The doctor saw that 90% of all the grafts had been blocked. The doctor called my surgeon as an emergency. He came rushing in in his shorts that looked like swimming shorts. He asked me what happened. I told him I had developed chest pain, which was more severe than before. He started working in his same clothing, on my angiogram.

He saw that I had developed keloids (irregular fibrous tissue formed at the site of a scar) causing thickening of skin. I was in great danger at that point. The doctor decided to try and do an angioplasty on the grafts. The angioplasties took about 25 minutes but the doctor took over three hours to do the procedure. It was done and I was taken to the CCU (cardiac care unit) for recovery. I did not have anesthesia so when I arrived at the CCU, I was shivering with the catheter still in my groin because during the procedures, they injected lots of blood thinner. I had to sleep in one position and I was told not to move my right leg. The nurse checked my groin every 30 minutes. It was painful I kept shivering. At about 1 AM, the nurse checked and took the catheter out, putting a small plaster. Praise the Lord; I was getting a little warm at that time. I slept well after that and woke up when breakfast came. I was taken to the general ward for the doctor to examine me. The doctor was satisfied and sent me home.

Come to think of these incidents, why I was in right place at right time and how were the doctors available at the weekend to save me? I was saved by His grace.

Third Heart Attack

In May 1996, on a Saturday, my wife and I were shopping at OK Bazaar supermarket, in Francistown. I had discomfort in my chest. I did not say anything but reached home with our grocery. I was very tired so I lay on the bed for rest but I had chest pain. I knew that it was my heart problem. I took an aspirin and placed a Nitro tablet under my tongue.

My wife called my friend Jivanbhai to drive me to the hospital. He came immediately and took me to the emergency room. There, a Bangladeshi doctor checked me and said that there was no problem. I had no heart issues.

We returned home. But in the evening, I had more chest pain. There was no time to wait, so I drove to the hospital with my wife. The doctor hospitalized me for the chest pain. I was put in a private ward, in a single room. I thought I would have good service because there was no other patient except me. In the morning, at about 4 AM, I had severe chest pain. So I called the nurse but she was not there. No one was seen at the special ward. I had my Nitro tablet so I placed one under my tongue. I was feeling a little better. I took some water and waited for someone to come. There were no phone services in the ward, neither were there any cellphones in those days.

At 9 AM, Dr. Horn came to check on the patients. He came to my room and saw me. He knew me well. He was surprised to see me in the ward and asked me what happened to me. I told him about my chest pain. Immediately, he took action and admitted me to ICU and connected all necessary instruments. There were no adequate facilities for heart problems. Dr. Horn arranged for a mercy flight to fly me to Johannesburg, South Africa. The business community gathered in a big crowd to see me.

We were only four of us in the mercy flight. I was on oxygen in the flight; my wife was massaging my head, sitting by me. A nurse was taking care of me and then there was the pilot. We reached Johannesburg airport at about 9 PM. From there, an ambulance took us to the hospital.

At the hospital's entrance, my friend Amin Sardar's wife Khatija was waiting for us. She made all the necessary documentation and my wife was comforted. She took my wife to her house. She kept her like her own sister. Khatija was of good help. She brought my wife to visit me every day. The house was in the same neighborhood as the hospital.

The doctor took me to the operation theater for my angiogram. After that, he inserted the angioplasty balloon inside the graft. I was in the hospital for four days and then we returned home to Francistown.

Two months later:

On 20th July 1996, I was in Johannesburg on a business meeting with the chain group of buyers. I left my wife at our friend's house. I left early to get to the office before the meeting started. Our meeting was at 10 AM and I reached at about 8.30 AM. So, we decided to go to a restaurant for breakfast. I'd already had my breakfast but joined them to be together for the meeting. At the restaurant, water glasses were served and I took the first sip. I had a problem swallowing the water. I did not say anything. I didn't take any breakfast. At 10 AM, the meeting started and we were successful. So, the three of us went for lunch. For lunch, I ordered salad. The other two ordered salads, too. We started eating and I started choking but I still did not mention it to anyone. I could not eat but asked for a cup of coffee. I drank a little coffee.

From the restaurant, I drove straight to my cardiologist. Johannesburg is a very big city. It's like New York's Manhattan. I drove through the heavy traffic.

The cardiologist was available. He checked me and asked me to go to the hospital for further tests. The hospital was within the area.

While going to the hospital, I called my friend's house and told them that I was at the hospital for tests.

My friend Amin Sardar, his wife Khatija and my wife came rushing. I was taken to the operation theater for another angiogram. We were supposed to wait in Johannesburg to receive our little daughter Sylvia, who was coming from the USA for her vacation.

The doctor was very sympathetic towards me and said that I had to go for a by-pass surgery for the second time. This was not planned so it came as a shock to all of us. I was admitted to the Mil-Park hospital. Sylvia arrived the same evening. She was worried, too, but it was good that she was there to comfort my wife.

Two days later, I had the surgery. I was not worried this time but both Sylvia and my wife were worried about the situation.

My surgery was done successfully, but I was kept in the hospital for one week because I lived about 1000 km away from Johannesburg. The doctor was my good friend because I was partners with his Jewish friend.

I was discharged from the hospital on 29 July 1996. My Swiss friend Mr. Hans Fischer came to see me at the hospital. He flew from Francistown to Johannesburg just to visit me. He saw that I was discharged, so he waited one more day and accompanied me and took good care of me. He took me with him on the flight to Francistown.

My health was deteriorating. I returned to my normal duties but I could not bear the work tension. The business was going well but I was not in a good condition.

My primary doctor told me not to get into any arguments with anyone. In business, we had to get into arguments every day. Besides business problems, I had to deal with the labor department, I had labor union confrontations, the tax department, getting raw materials, manufacturing in time, delivering goods on the negotiated date, wage-related wars, price wars and so many other business problems that I could not remain in good shape.

I resigned from the board of directors. I withdrew my personal guarantees given to the bank.

In 1998, I started selling my assets and prepared to retire. I had lots of losses but I sold everything at give-away prices and returned to India for retirement. In India, we stayed for about 17 months.

Our children wanted us to join them in the USA. We had our Green Card and all the valid documents.

When our first grandson, Nicholas, was born, we were all excited. We decided to go to the USA.

We went to the USA and lived with our older daughter Angelina and her husband Sanjay. We took care of our first grandson.

That was our first babysitting job.

Our son-in-law was very pleased that we went to take care of them. He took us to the Calvary Chapel of Hope in Long Island, where we started learning the Bible. The church and Sanjay gave us good Bible knowledge.

At the church, on the first day, the book of Revelation was started. It was a blessing for us because we had very little knowledge of the book. We had daily devotion-time at home, with Sanjay. I began feeling that the Lord was drawing us to a new life with Biblical knowledge.

My wife and I worked very hard in our life—first for our family in India and later for our children in Botswana. God led us all the way, though narrow and rugged ways but now, He had made our life peaceful and happy, during our retirement. His ways are rough, narrow and painful but they lead to happiness at the end.

Arriving in the USA was easy because our children were already educated and had earned doctorate degrees there. They were married and had happy lives.

The blessing of our Lord was flowing on us, at all times. After our daughter Sylvia graduated with a DMD from Pennsylvania University, we arranged for her marriage. Our Lord did all that which happened in our lives. We did not have to go and arrange her marriage. The proposal came from a family from my wife's hometown.

Dr. Emanuel Christian, a theologian with good Bible knowledge, and his wife, Violet, wrote Biblical books. They approached us with a marriage proposal for their son, Samir. He was a well-educated boy with good standing in his work. He met Sylvia and both accepted to join in matrimony. The marriage took place in New York, at Angelina and Sanjay's house, with the help of his family. We are blessed. The marriage ceremonies went well and our youngest daughter, Sylvia, was married.

My Church Life

Rt. Rev. Shannon Mallory was the first Bishop of Botswana. Before he came to Botswana, we had a steering committee meeting at Serowe, Botswana, to form the Diocese of Botswana. I was on that committee. Botswana was Bechuanaland, which was a South Africa protectorate country. The British government gave power to the South African government to manage the country because most of the country comprised of the Kalahari Desert. Bechuanaland Anglican Church was under the Diocese of South Africa. But after Bechuanaland became a free country under the name of Botswana, we formed the Diocese of Botswana, detaching from South Africa.

After becoming an independent Diocese, the other Central-African countries joined us.

Our Bishop became in-charge of four Dioceses—Botswana, Zambia, Zimbabwe and Malawi. I was nominated as Northern Botswana's treasurer. The treasurer of the Diocese was Mr. Bakwena. The Northern Botswana Diocese was not doing well and could not even pay all the dues.

One day, our Bishop Rt. Rev. Mallory stood at the gate of the church and I was at the door of the church; it was a Sunday. He loudly said that he declared the Francistown Parish bankrupt. I was furious and shouted back at him and I challenged him. I asked him to hand over all the administration of the Northern chapter to us and that I would show him how we did better than his Parish. He laughed and said that it was my baby from then on. I accepted it and started working on my accounts. I was a businessman with good accounting knowledge. In one months' time, I changed the whole scenario and started paying the Diocese's dues on time. We paid our priest from our account. In three months, we had surplus money in the bank. The Bishop did not know that. At the standing committee meeting, I was asked to give the treasurer's report. I showed a huge balance on the balance sheet. He was shocked and asked me how I'd managed that.

I gave him all my records and he named me as 'Northern Botswana's Mafia.' He then came to our parish and we had the AGM (Annual General meeting).

He humbly asked me to hand over the Parish back to him because the Parish had a good income. The Lord guides us to do all kinds of work. He showed me the way. He infused ideas in my mind. I rented our church to a Bible class after our services were over. They paid a rent of Pula 400. (Pula is Botswana's Currency)

I moved our priest to our local church area's newly-built house, near a Setswana language service in St. Carantoc's Church. The English service was at St. Patrick's Church in the city. I moved our priest, Father Duiker, to the local people's location.

The Baptist Mission, by mistake, built a house on our church land so I claimed the house. He had to hand over the house's keys to me with the agreement that I pay for the building a very small amount. I moved Father Duiker to the newly-built, spacious house. Now, our Parish had one more property as our capital. The city's house was old but it was very big and in the middle of the residential area. I renovated the house quickly and rented it out. The income was booming for us and we paid all out dues and stipend to our Priest better than what the Diocese paid him. The Diocese took over the Francistown Administration from us. I handed over the bank account to Gaborone head office.

Other reasons for handing over to Diocese were personal to me—it was that I was having heart issues and I was too busy developing my own business. This was the Lord's guidance. He blessed me and gave me all the ideas to develop St. Patrick's Church, the Northern Botswana Parish of Diocese of Botswana.

I had good standing in the Anglican Church of the Diocese of Botswana.

Hunting Is Fun (a Mistake)

We were in the jungle with lots of wild animals around us. We traveled about 25 miles from our town area to find animals. We were about 10 of us—all businessmen. We used to go for long weekends in the jungle for game hunting. We had to have a guide with us—a man from the department of wildlife. We had to get permits to hunt animals mentioned on the permit—like, one Giraffe, one elephant, two wildebeests and all of the antelope family. We were not professional hunters, so we did not go for big animals like giraffes, elephants or buffalo. We mainly hunted wildebeest, springbuck, Impala and Kudu. We had to get permission to target the animal from the guide because, during certain months, we could not kill female animals.

One day, when I was hunting in Maun area near Moremi game reserve, I did not find any animal. We found animals like lion and Zebras but they were not our choice. I was an army-trained soldier so I had good practice in shooting with rifles. One of my friends registered a rifle on my name. If the gun was not registered on my name, I could not shoot. We were all tired hunting in the heat of Kalahari Desert's wilderness. I sat on the spare wheel of my Land Rover. I started hunting Guniea-fowls and Pheasants. I had a good time shooting over 200 birds on that day. The villagers in the jungle wanted the birds. We gave them all the birds.

One day, we were in the Lubang area of the desert, which is near Serowe, the village of Sir Seretse Khama—the first President of Botswana. We usually camped in the jungle and lit a huge campfire and slept around the fire. Two of the helpers had night duty to keep the fire alive. Once the fire died down, the animals start coming to us while we were sleeping. Animals like the Hyena and Lion were dangers in the Kalahari Desert. In the morning, when we woke up, my neighboring man picked up his sleeping bag and found a snake under it. We saw the snake— it was a Black Mamba. Black Mamba snakes were very common in Southern Africa. If it bit a person, he could die in minutes. We killed small animals that day. Usually, we had all the animals cleaned up in the jungle itself and the workers make biltong of wild animals' meat, with salt and pepper and dried them on a line. The Kalahari Desert is usually very hot during the daytime, so we got biltong made in a couple of days.

On one of the trips, we had a bad experience. We were in the Makgadikgadi pan, which is a saltpan because of the rock salt sediments. Animals licked the salt and usually, in the area, the animals were fat. We were hunting in the area and one of the Land Rovers left a little earlier than our Land Rover. We were still in the camp, having our breakfast. We left half an hour after as we were in an area that we all knew. We drove for about one hour but did not find the first group. After hours of searching, we found that the group's vehicle had fallen in a big hole. They managed to come out of the hole but the vehicle was still inside, and it was difficult to pull it out. We walked miles to find some small trees that we could use as a wedge to pull the Land Rover out of the hole. We worked very hard getting trees from a mile away because, in the saltpan, there were no trees. The hole was made by local Bushmen to trap elephants. We had a hard time pulling the vehicle out from the trap. We were thirsty, hungry and tired working in the heat of the Kalahari Desert. We managed to pull the vehicle out by 6 PM. We reached our camp at about 7 PM. We did not hunt anything the whole day. The next day, we were very careful and hunted only bucks for Biltong.

My best experience was in the area north of Maun, near the Caprivi Strip area. We saw a few impalas but they were behind an anthill. One colored man whom we brought for cleaning animals jumped out of the vehicle, which was not allowed. He walked slowly behind the animals. After about 15 minutes, he did not return so we starting searching for him. We started circling the area but he was not found for a long time. It was hot, dry and difficult to wait in the vehicle. We kept our car window open to hear his call. But he was not to be found. There were no cellphones in those days. After about more than two hours of search, we heard a bird singing. I was sitting on the spare wheel in front of the vehicle. We kept silent to hear the sound. We drove in the direction of the whistling. As soon as we reached near the tree, he jumped out of the tree and started crying.

He was sweating and tired. He grabbed one gallon of water and drank it very fast.

In the national park, we were warned not to come out of the vehicle, but some people do not listen.

On that day, I had a good chance of shooting a full-blooded wildebeest. It was standing in front of me, about 20 feet away from our vehicle. When you find any animal, you cannot shoot from your vehicle. That is the rule of the department of wildlife. I took aim and shot the animal under the chin. It was a heart shot and I managed to kill the animal instantly. After that, the man who got stranded in the morning also found another animal and he shot another wild beast. This was a female animal, and it was suffering. The workers started killing the animal and found that the female was with fold. I saw the baby coming out of the mother.

It was not nice to see that we kill the life thinking that it's fun but it was killing a life. I was restless that day and made up my mind to not go hunting anymore.

I had forgotten the Ten Commandments during my young age itself, living among the unbelievers. That particular incident was printed on my mind, and it did not allow me to hold any weapon at any time. I cannot repent enough though the killing of that particular animal was not my job.

American Life

We were the only Gujarati Christian family in Botswana. The children were growing. They were doing their secondary education, so I had to think about their future. We were worried about our children. My brother, Augustine, had filed an immigration petition for us. The Lord was gracious to us at all the time. Just before our son George completed his high school graduation, we were given a visa call from the American Embassy Gaborone, Botswana. We completed all the required documentation and we made arrangements to travel to the USA.

We immigrated to the USA with a Green Card so our son could do his further schooling. He was admitted in UCLA College for his Bachelor degree. He lived with my brother, Augustine. After two years, our daughters joined their brother and lived with Augustine and Manorama. Both Augustine and Manorama kept them like their own children.

After a while, Augustine found a condo for our children, so we could move in together. The condo was in Granada Hills, San Fernando Valley, Los Angeles. Augustine also bought a car for our children. George was all set for his studies. He was doing well in his studies. The three lived and educated themselves in colleges. God helped us, making our way easy. We were in Botswana because we could not wind up our affairs in Africa immediately.

Our children had lots of difficulties, as we could not send money to them, because of the exchange control regulation. I could send only half of my income to my children. We had to get letters from the colleges that our children were in their schools to get permission to send money for their requirements. I had business friends who helped me occasionally. I used to get connections to get money transferred to USA. Our children were disciplined and did not spend money but concentrated on their studies. This was also a blessing of our Lord.

Angelina moved to UC San Francisco Pharmacy College. At that time, our second daughter found a school in UC Riverside College, LA. And our son was doing his studies for medical school (UCLA). When he graduated and was about to move to Missouri for medical college, he came to Botswana for a visit. We had a good time with him. After a short stay in Botswana, he returned to US and landed at San Francisco to meet his sister, Angelina.

The next day, he came to Los Angeles and had his dinner at Augustine's home. After that, he returned to his condo in Granada Hills, San Fernando Valley.

He was tired travelling so he went to bed early. He slept but early in the morning, there was an earthquake. In 1994, the earthquake was in Northridge area, where my son's condo was. Our condo was completely destroyed. Our son was sleeping, but he heard the big sound so he woke up and found himself under the room's ceiling. The ceiling collapsed and was just over him. He was in deep sleep and did not know what was going on. He saw the condo's side door open so he walked out, still in his sleep.

It was raining at that time. So, he came to his senses after getting wet. He picked up his suitcase quickly and jumped in his car, which was still safe. He drove to Augustine's house. Fortunately, he turned right at the highway to go to Moorpark. The left side of the highway was broken and a policeman had driven straight into the hole early in the morning, at 4 AM, and died.

Fortunately, all our children had completed their studies and did not need the condo anymore. President Clinton did mention that the government would compensate for the damages, but we were away in Africa and the children were at their colleges.

We lost the condo and all the money spent. I went to the bank and argued that the loan was given to us with fully comprehensive insurance, but the manager said that we did not have 'act of God' insurance. I did not know about the existence of such a type of insurance. I asked what comprehensive meant. He mentioned it fully covered everything but for natural disasters. I had to give up my condo and all the hard-earned money was gone with it.

Soon after our daughter Angelina graduated from her medical college, we arranged for her marriage with a devotional family and God blessed us with our son-in-law, Sanjay. We travelled to and fro New York from Los Angeles, to find her a match from her choice of boys of Christian backgrounds and from our communities. The Lord was with us so with very little difficulty, we found her a match. Angelina was soon married with the help of Augustine and his wife Manorama. Without their support and love, we would not have tasted such success.

Soon after that, I had heart problems and I went for my second by-pass surgery. I was weak and very sick. I could not concentrate on my work and had lots of work tension. I was told by my physician to stop working, stop meetings and stop any arguments in business. I was doing that every day. I had to make a decision. The children wanted us to move from Africa.

At that time, our son George was about to graduate from medical college. Before graduation, he was supposed to have medical experiences out of America. We suggested to him to come to India and attend medical college in India. He did that in Ahmadabad because we were there in 1997/98. We arranged his marriage and asked him to select a girl he liked. He made his decision but he said he wanted to complete his education first. After he was done with his studies, he told us about his choice of a girl in India. He got married to Teena Baraiya in Ahmadabad. After that, he graduated from medical college as a Doctor. After marriage, when his wife Teena came to America and joined him in Missouri, he had his family with him and decided to study further. He became a physician in Internal Medicine in Chicago and thence, with hard work, he became a Gastroenterologist in Michigan. Our son had lots of difficulties in going through his goal, but he was blessed with a good wife and good education.

We are a happy family with three grandchildren in New York, two grandchildren in New Hampshire and one grandson in Tennessee. Three dimensions completed the trinity, with the Lord with us. Praise the Lord, George and Teena have one additional gift of God, a daughter, Elaina. Our Seventh grandchild, the complete number according to the Bible.

My Work in USA

When we arrived in USA, I still had not regained my health. We lived at our daughter's home in Long Island, New York. I could not get a job because of my health history and my age factor. I realized that I would have to remain fully retired. We lived in New York with Angelina and Sanjay because their children were small. We were babysitting. After three years, when Sylvia was married, she moved to New Hampshire. Sylvia and Samir called us to come and stay with them because their first child was about to be born.

We moved to New Hampshire and kept ourselves busy by taking care of little Nicole. I was learning to use the computer and reading books. I kept busy by working the whole day.

At that time, I had a call from Angelina that someone from Washington was looking for me.

She gave my phone number to the person. I had a call for US Aid, through International Executive Service Corp. (IESC). I was surprised and asked them how they got my contact. They said that they had my profile and found me.

They asked me to go to Africa for IESC. (International Executive Service Corp.) I asked for details of the assignment to evaluate.

Anyway, I was assigned to go to Africa for three weeks. I was assigned to visit factories in Kenya, Tanzania, Rwanda/Burundi, Madagascar and lastly in Moshi/Arusha.

It was a new experience for me, doing an executive's job for the USA's government. It was a volunteer job, on per-diem basis.

I accepted the offer and took up the challenge. I was given top-class treatment, full US government security, a car and a driver and five-star hotel accommodation. I was meeting US Embassy officers in various countries. The interpreters wherever needed—like French-speaking countries.

The government's travel agent sent tickets from Washington for the various places and countries with hotel accommodations and transfers.

The US government's travel agent arranged bookings for people to receive me at the airports to take me to the hotel, for special executive suite for meetings at the hotel, including all meals.

I started my work tour to Africa. I knew the continent, and most of the languages were known to me, too.

I landed first at Amsterdam, where I had to halt for half a day. I was tired already so I took a shower there, changed into different clothing and embarked on my journey to Kenya. At Nairobi airport, a company's personnel received me. Nairobi was not a new city for me. I'd visited the city several times for business.

At the hotel, I met the foreign minister of Zambia and had a good talk on trade, at the breakfast table. He invited me to go to Zambia. I met another interesting person, the director of East African Airways; he was sitting with his group so he introduced me to the group. At the executive lounge, there were many foreign personnel. They were from CPA (Caribbean, Pacific and Africa) countries.

After breakfast, a lady came looking for me. She was a coordinator to take me around to the places of interest. The first day, we went to the US Embassy to meet the High Commissioner casually. Then, I met with the First Secretary and Trade Attaché' to discuss President Bush's 'AGOA' legislation. I had a lengthy discussion on tariffs for the duty-free export of African products to the US.

I visited a businessman who was on my list. His factory was in Mombasa, about 300 miles from Nairobi. He was a cabinet minister of the central government. He showed me his products, samples and prices. His factory was not mass-producing goods. I had to be in Nairobi and the next day I was supposed to visit some traditional manufacturers. It was amazing what people did without modern technology.

The next day, I flew to Madagascar. I was flying to Antananarivo. The name is very long so the local people called it Tanna.

At Tanna, there were problems in communicating with the Immigration officer because they spoke French or Kriol (broken French) but fortunately, a lady from USA saw me struggling, came to me and helped me get my visa at the airport. She asked me what I was doing in Madagascar. I told her that I was there through USAID. She introduced herself to me and said that she was working with the US Embassy. I was lucky to meet the right person at the airport. She invited me to come to her office.

My transport was waiting for me to take me to the City hotel. I asked her to join me because she was looking for a taxi.

She came with me and while talking to her, I saw some strange formation of clouds; I saw Jesus on the lap of Mary. I was looking for my camera but it was at the backseat of the car. In a short while, I saw Jesus hanging on a cross. These formations of clouds were very strange and fascinating. I thought to myself that Jesus was there to take care of those people. I passed by a slum area of Madagascar. People seemed very poor and their living standards were really bad.

We reached the Hilton Hotel of Antananarivo. It was a special accommodation—a secure room for me. I rested for the day and met a gentleman from Germany, who'd come to build infrastructure. We had a good talk about Madagascar and the people. He gave me a good idea about the standard of living of the local people.

In the evening, however, a lady came to meet me. She was an interpreter assigned to me because Madagascar was a French colony. The following morning, a car came with the interpreter and the manager of a company, which I was supposed to visit.

I had to visit the clothing factory and improve their products and improve the cost of production.

At the factory, the owner's wife was the in-charge of the business. She introduced me to the supervisory staff. I started working with the floor manager. I started with the cutting section and found lots of mistakes in the section. They used to use lots of fabric to cut dresses. I showed them how to lay the patterns on the layers. The fabric for the top part of the clothing was wasted. I showed them to cut 24 dresses from the fabric they used to cut a couple of dresses. I asked the supervisor to cut 24 dresses out of that fabric. They tried my way but cut only 22 tops of dresses.

All the workers from the cutting section came to the owner's office and said that they had cut 22 only. The owner was very angry with them because they had been wasting so much fabric that the cost of the product could not match up to the competitors in the market. The cutting section's staff, the owner and the manager were amazed to see such saving at the beginning of my visit itself.

Then, in the sewing section, I noticed that the workers were uncomfortable with me because they feared that I might find their mistakes, too. I showed the owner that the stitching was good but not up to the standard. I showed them their problem areas and they were very happy to see that I'd found their problems and that they could save 45% of cost and quality of the clothing. They gave me some clothing as gifts for my grandchildren, Nicholas and Sarah. Now, they could stand and compete in the USA market with confidence.

They were so pleased that the next day, Saturday morning, as I was having my breakfast, they came to the hotel and said that they wanted to take me out for a day's tour in Madagascar. I had been of much help to their company.

I was unaware of the trip but then, I saw one special car brought for me to travel with the owners of the company. Their brother-in-law was the driver and a bus followed the car with the office staff and all the supervisors. About 20 of them had come just to receive me. I was shocked to see their gesture and joined them for the tour.

They showed me the village life, hut industries with semi-precious stones like Ruby, Malachite and all kinds and colors of stones—diamonds too! I was not sure about the quality and genuineness of the stones because it was a primitive place. The people who traveled with me told me that it was genuine. I bought some stones. I saw so many amazing places. The beauty of Madagascar was such that I wish to go there again someday.

The next day, the personnel from the US Embassy came to visit me at the hotel. They were concentrating more on agriculture. The lady from the embassy and a local agricultor accompanied her. We had coffee together and had a good chat about exports from Madagascar. She gave me some idea of the big businesses of Madagascar.

On Monday, I visited a Clothing industry which was on my agenda. The factory was doing a good job but it was not well-organized. They had costing problems. I had to work sorting the work place and took half a day doing the costing. We could not finish the work because they did not have certain documents. I had to go to the office the next day for finishing the work. The documents required for dispatching to USA and Bank Letter of Credit requirement was explained. They were very happy with my visit. In the evening, they entertained me by taking me to a nice restaurant for seafood; they took me around the city and showed me the Presidential palace! I had a great trip to Madagascar.

From Madagascar, I had to return to Nairobi. The flight was going via Zanzibar and I was much interested in seeing the city of Zanzibar—the island I'd visited on my voyage from India to Africa in 1955. The modern Zanzibar was a very charming place with lots of beaches, hotels and tourist attractions.

I reached Nairobi and relaxed in the hotel. I had a night in Nairobi but I was not allowed to go out of the hotel because of security reasons. I met a few Indians who were residents of Nairobi. They'd come to play at the casino.

The following day, I flew to Rwanda/Burundi. Rwanda is an untouched beauty. Its capital city, Kigali, is built on a thousand hills. Though they had great genocide in the country, the country seemed very quiet. People were good and business areas were normal.

The manager of a full-fledged textile industry came to pick me up and show me the factory. I was impressed with the production. Though some of the areas of the factory were not in operation, the factory was into mass production. They were producing Police and Army uniforms. When I visited the factory, the army's clothing was in mass production. The workers were very skilled and the quality of the garments was very good. They had no clothing for exports to the USA.

The country shares its border with Uganda, where Volcano National park is located. Giant-sized Gorillas were found there. The surrounding villages' population was producing traditional products—they were marvelous. It was heart-breaking looking at such a beautiful country and such good people undergoing genocide.

Tribal wars and political wars are two of the worst enemies of innocent mankind.

From Kigali, I flew back to Nairobi and had a good night's rest. The next morning, I had the opportunity to visit the traditional market. It was unthinkable and amazing to see what people produced from raw material. They produced furniture from railway sleepers, animal skin and many other raw materials.

From Nairobi, I flew to Moshi/Arusha of Tanzania—the place of the famous Kilimanjaro Mountain, Ngoro-Ngoro creator and Serengeti National

Park. I saw many national parks in Africa but on this trip, I saw the Kilimanjaro while driving through it. I had seen the Kilimanjaro from my airplane about four times but this time, I went driving around it.

In Arusha, Tanzania, I was assigned to see a clothing factory. The factory was big and production was good. I was impressed with the production of the company. The owner was not there so the manager showed me the operations. I had a good talk with the Director over the phone about their products being marketed in USA. He was excited about it but did not have much production to meet the market needs of the USA. I saw that the factory was very good and production was of good quality. There were some stitching and cutting-section problems, which I suggested that they improve. The workers were very skilled and the quality of the garments was excellent.

From Moshi airport, I flew to Dar Es' Salaam. I did not have any business in Dar Es' Salaam, but I met some business contacts, which I had in the past. The next evening, I had to fly back to the USA via Amsterdam.

That was 10 landings and 10 takeoffs in three weeks. It was hard work and the journeys were tiring, but I was rewarded with a Presidential Award for a job well done.

I had to represent all the African manufacturers at the ASAP Global trade show and MAGIC trade show. I worked as the matchmaking personnel for those African businesses. Every six months, I had to go to Las Vegas as a representative for Africa and worked at the trade show for one week. I worked for two years as a matchmaker, for African industries to find buyers in USA.

I was thinking about all this work. How could all this happen to me—that I was employed—without even applying for jobs? I had gone blank during my retirement. I was very busy in my work in Africa and suddenly, I was without job, without Phone, Fax or any business—but the Lord opened this avenue for me to get involved in doing something that interested me.

After the US Aid job, I was busy contacting my clients and the office in Washington and Nairobi. It was not very rewarding work but it was the Lord's grace that I was put in a business, which kept me busy and very-much-alive.

'It is no secret what God can do.'

Through Jesus Christ, we have everything we need for life and godliness 2 Peter, 1–3. With God's help, we can move past our self-centered ways to carry out God's plan, glory and goodness

THE END.

CPSIA information can be obtained
at www.ICGtesting.com
Printed in the USA
LVHW050803270723
753093LV00003B/344

9 781645 879688